THE
MAKING OF AMERICA
SERIES

MARITIME
MARION
MASSACHUSETTS

Sheds for shucking scallops line Island Wharf during a 1930s scallop season. Sheds were also used to store gear.

THE
MAKING OF AMERICA
SERIES

MARITIME MARION
MASSACHUSETTS

JUDITH WESTLUND ROSBE

ARCADIA

Published by Arcadia Publishing,
an imprint of Tempus Publishing, Inc.
2 Cumberland Street
Charleston, SC 29401

Printed in Great Britain.
Library of Congress Catalog Card Number: 2001095849

For all general information contact Arcadia Publishing at:
Telephone 843-853-2070
Fax 843-853-0044
E-Mail sales@arcadiapublishing.com

For customer service and orders:
Toll-Free 1-888-313-2665

Visit us on the Internet at http://www.arcadiapublishing.com

*For my grandson Augustinius George Vrattos,
who was born December 15, 2000.*

Popeye *is the beloved miniature tug at Barden's Boat Yard.*

CONTENTS

ACKNOWLEDGMENTS

This book began when Jack Braitmayer, a longtime Marion resident, suggested to Jim Weinberg, a director of the Sippican Historical Society, that the society should write a maritime history of Marion because of the community's unique relationship with the sea throughout its more than 300-year existence. Jim passed the suggestion on to me, a fellow director of the Sippican Historical Society since 1978 and a past president for nine years, because he knew of my avid interest in Marion's history. I readily took up the gauntlet. Jack Braitmayer has assisted me throughout this project, and I am most grateful to him for his encouragement.

There were many others who helped me along the way: Richard A. Anderson, Richard I. Arthur, David B. Barker, Charles Bascom, Mary Jean Blasdale, Charles Brown, H. Peter Converse, Michael Cudahy, Michael P. Dyer, Samuel A. Francis, the late Thayer Francis Jr., Stuart M. Frank, William Gilkerson, Gordon L. Goodwin, Llewellyn Howland III, Robert B. Jones, John and Nancy Kendall, Trudy Kingery, Judith Kleven, Joyce Kohout, Peter H. McCormick, Frank McNamee, Tracy Tortora McNeil, Bryan J. McSweeney, Seth Mendell, Michael J. Moore, John J. Palmieri, Laura Pereira, Bill and Tinker Saltonstall, David W. Schloerb, Wendy W. Schnur, Jean Fraser Spader, Robert R. Thompson, the Sippican Historical Society, the Marion Public Library, the Kendall Whaling Museum, the New Bedford Whaling Museum, the Public Archaeology Lab, the Mystic Seaport Museum, the Herreshoff Marine Museum, Tabor Academy, Sippican, Inc., and my husband, Bob Rosbe, who read each and every draft and shared his extensive yacht design library with me. I am continually amazed and overwhelmed by their kindness and generosity.

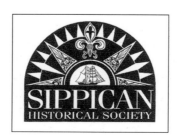

INTRODUCTION

Located on the southeast coast of Massachusetts, the Town of Marion is 60 miles south of Boston, 20 miles southwest of Plymouth—where the Pilgrims first landed in America—and 11 miles east of New Bedford, once the whaling capital of America. A small town, Marion has only 4,901 year-round residents, but in the summer its population grows to 7,180. It covers approximately 14 square miles with 25 miles of coastline.

Though Marion was originally inhabited by the Sippican Indians, a community of the Wampanoag tribe, Pilgrim families from Plymouth Plantation settled what is present-day Marion in 1678. The first settlement was at Little Neck at the head of Sippican Harbor, a site especially rich in clams. To this day, many fine restaurants refer to the smallest hard-shell clams as "littlenecks."

Marion later broke away from Rochester and in 1852 was incorporated as a separate town. Its residents chose the name Marion to honor a Revolutionary War hero from South Carolina, Francis Marion, whose guerrilla warfare tactics were admired by the "coasting captains" who delivered salt to South Carolina in exchange for white oak brought back for shipbuilding. These men preferred the name Marion to the area's Native American name Sippican, which means "the long river."

Thanks to its seaside location, Marion has a wonderfully rich maritime history. Beginning with the first settlement at Little Neck in the late seventeenth century, when Marion was part of Rochester-Towne, the community's economy centered on shipbuilding, whaling, fishing, and salt making. These industries also remained important throughout the eighteenth and nineteenth centuries despite the challenges that then arose.

When England put a heavy duty on salt during the Revolutionary War, Yankee ingenuity took over. In 1829, more salt was manufactured by means of the solar evaporation of seawater in Rochester than anywhere else in the region. Also, the ship registers for the customs district of New Bedford record that more ships (183) were built in Rochester from 1782 to 1850 than in the much larger port of New Bedford, which during the same period built 133.

During the late nineteenth and early twentieth centuries, Marion became popular as a summer resort where rich and famous visitors enjoyed yachting, recreational fishing, and the town's beaches, thanks mostly to Richard Watson Gilder, who purchased a run-down stone building and converted it into a studio for his artist wife and their famous friends.

Marion's seaside location also attracted maritime-related industries in the twentieth century such as the Marconi Wireless Telegraph Company, which had a station in Marion, and Sippican, Inc., makers of instrumentation and other products for the oceanographic market.

Marion also boasts Tabor Academy, an independent secondary school on the harbor. The school ties many of its educational and sports programs to the sea, and for this it has earned national acclaim. Likewise, the Beverly Yacht Club in Marion trains young sailors, sponsors racing for small boats and large yachts, and hosts the bi-annual Marion-to-Bermuda Cruising Yacht Race.

This book pays tribute to Marion's rich maritime history as the town celebrates its sesquicentennial in 2002.

Sippican Harbor is pictured here c. 1955.

1. Historical Overview

The geology of the land around Marion was created by the alternating ebb and flow of a massive ice sheet during the Pleistocene Ice Age, which ended approximately 12,000 years ago. This ice sheet carried glacial till consisting of silt, sand, gravel, and stone that ultimately formed the ridges of Marion's coastline. It also created Great Hill, which at 124 feet above sea level is the highest point in Marion. Glacial melt created interior wetlands such as Bear Swamp in the northwest part of town and enabled the development of extensive cranberry bogs on the northern end of Sippican Neck in more recent times.

Buzzards Bay borders Marion to the east and south, and the majority of coastal rivers, fed by the wetlands and running from north to south, empties into the bay. Marion also contains three peninsulas extending into the sea: Converse Point (originally called Charles Neck), Sippican Neck, and Great Hill, which extend from the mainland into the bay, flanking Sippican Harbor and its inlets, Aucoot Cove, Hammetts Cove, and Wings Cove. Little Neck is located at the head of Sippican Harbor.

Archaeologists believe that Marion was inhabited more than 12,000 years ago. Its residents were probably clustered along the coast and around wetlands because of the kinds of plant and animal species that were supported in those areas. Prehistoric sites are generally found in areas of sandy soils near wetlands, streams, and coastal settings. Having documented 10,000 years of human occupation in the area that is now home to Marion's residents, archaeologists assert that from 5,500 to 3,000 B.C. there was regular harvesting of anadromous fish and various plants, which was combined with hunting. They have found evidence of regular shellfish exploitation during the period from 3,000 to 1,000 B.C. in areas close to swamps, marshes, tidal flats, streams, and major rivers. From 1,000 B.C. to 300 A.D., little is known of the social organization or economy of this area because of the scarcity of items found by archaeologists. It was during this period of time, however, that pottery was first made. From 300 to 1500 A.D., the economy in Marion focused on coastal resources as is evidenced by the shell middens and stone artifacts of this period found in coastal areas.

Native Americans settled around streams and wetlands, which provided a home and breeding habitat for animals, as well as food for themselves (wild cranberries thrive in this area). From 1500 to 1620, Native Americans such as the Wampanoag, a name that means "People of the First Light," were settled in the land around Sippican Harbor under the leadership of Chief Massasoit. Numerous villages and seasonal camps were connected by a network of ancient trails that followed the coast. Native Americans fished and harvested shellfish in these waters, and favorable fishing locations were visited annually, as they had been for many generations. They did on-shore fishing and ate whales that washed up on beaches (drift whales) during the seventeenth century. They also fished using hand-lines, weirs near the shore, and small craft. The coastal Wampanoags also engaged in commerce with European traders and fishermen, and descendants of the Wampanoags continued to live in the town of Marion once it had been established. Although their political, social, and economic organizations were relatively complex, the native people underwent rapid change during European colonization.

In 1602, the English explorer Bartholomew Gosnold became the first European to set foot in this area on Pekonoket (at Cuttyhunk). He also sailed up Buzzards Bay, which he called "Gosnold's Hope." Around 1610 a plague, probably smallpox carried by the first European explorers, descended upon the Wampanoags and wiped out many of the sub-tribes including the one that had established a summer camp at Plymouth, 20 miles to the northeast of present-day Marion. In 1615, the Penobscots of Maine attacked the Wampanoags, further reducing their numbers.

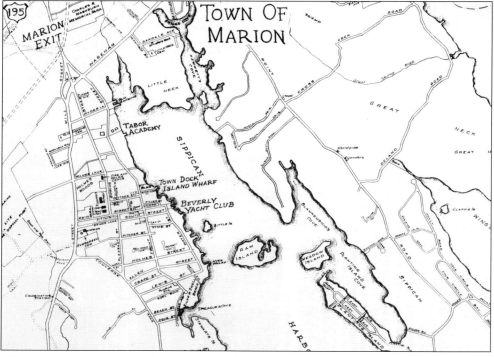

This map of Marion shows how it appears in the present.

A statue of Chief Massasoit by the American sculptor Cyrus Dallin stands on a Pilgrim burial ground in Plymouth, Massachusetts.

PLANTATION PERIOD: 1620–1675

The *Mayflower* arrived at Eastham near Provincetown on November 9, 1620. On December 16, after searching for a suitable location, the Pilgrims landed at Plymouth to begin their settlement. At the time of the founding of the Plymouth Plantation, present-day Marion was occupied by members of the Sippican community of the Wampanoag tribe. The main village was on Little Neck, a sandy promontory at the head of Sippican Harbor. It was oriented around a distinctive overhanging boulder formation, which is today called Minister's Rock, and included a native burial ground. A second settlement was located at Charles Neck on the west side of Sippican Harbor. Like Little Neck, this area featured a large, distinctive boulder (Charles Rock) and a burial ground. Additional settlements may have been located in the Great Hill area and at Aucoot Cove. Colonial sources described Native American meadows on Ram Island, near Great Hill, and elsewhere along the riverbanks and shoreline.

Minister's Rock at Little Neck was Reverend Shiverick's first pulpit in 1683. Before that, it was a prayer site for Sippican Indians as well as a burial ground.

The Puritan settlers who arrived at Plymouth Plantation in 1620 farmed and fished in order to survive. The settlers considered the establishment of a new plantation in present-day Marion as early as 1638, when a Sippican Plantation was offered to "eight men of Scituate for the benefit of the congregation of Reverend John Lothrup, who had fled from London." The offer was declined, although descendants of the group were among the first settlers in Sippican Village in present-day Marion years later.

In 1649, the Plymouth Colony General Court granted to the townsmen of Plymouth "eight miles by the sea and four miles into the land" at "Sepecan" as a place for the pasturage and wintering of cattle. Thus, beginning in 1649, the Pilgrims brought Plymouth Plantation's cattle to the lands of the Sippican Indians for winter pasturage. They found Sippican very much like their late home in England because of the oysters in the green salt marshes of the harbor and necks. By 1651, the Marion area had been mapped by Plymouth, and the boundaries of a Sippican Grant were formalized. The grant represented only a portion of the overall Sippican lands and was centered on the Sippican River and harbor of present-day Marion.

In 1655, the court at Plymouth authorized the purchase of "lands of the Indians of Sepecan to winter cattle on," and in 1660 two Plymouth agents were appointed "to sett the bounds of the lands granted to the towne of Plymouth att Sepecan." Massasoit, the sachem of the Wampanoags and friend of the English, died in 1661 and was succeeded by his eldest son, Wamsutta (Alexander). In June 1662,

Massasoit's other son, Philip, succeeded Alexander, whom he alleged was poisoned by the English. In 1666, King Philip empowered Watachpoo, sachem of the Sippicans, to authorize land sales to the English, and in 1688 he made a curious drawing (which has been preserved in the Plymouth Colony Records) to show the lands that might be sold. Most of the land he allowed to be sold, however, was useless swamp.

On July 11, 1667, the Native American known as Charles sold Charles Neck to the Rochester settlers for 6 pounds. In 1669, Joseph Bartlett, who had been improving the lands of Sepecan, agreed to pay the town of Plymouth 40 shillings for the use of these lands and to surrender the lease of the lands that he had held. In 1670, agents of the town of Plymouth also granted the Native American named Totosin (also called Tousand) the use of certain lands at Sippican and recorded their agreement about "a psell of Land desired by him att Sepecan" in the Plymouth town records.

In 1670, the General Court of Plymouth voted that the profits of the upland and meadow lands at "Agawam, Sepecan, and places adjacent" should be used for the support of a school at Plymouth, and in 1672–1673, agents from Plymouth colony were appointed to purchase "whatever lands are yet unpurchased of

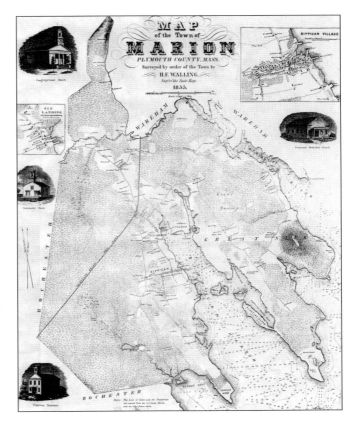

The first settlement in what would become Marion was at Little Neck at the head of Sippican Harbor in 1678. This map was result of a survey ordered by the town in 1855.

Plymouth graunt att Sepecan and places adjacent." It appears from the early records of the General Court of Plymouth that while various attempts were made by the colony and the town of Plymouth to purchase "the lands of Sepecan and places adjacent" and while certain tracts were actually purchased, no general purchase of these lands from the Native Americans was ever made.

When the last attempt at purchase was proposed in 1673, the Native American troubles were already beginning. Disagreements between the Native Americans and the Pilgrims led to King Philip's War, and waves of destruction were brought down upon the frontier settlements by Philip's forces. The western floodplain of the Sippican River in present-day northern Marion was set aside as a forced internment area for Native American non-combatants. Watachpoo was made a prisoner on his own land after being accused of conspiring with King Philip. The death of King Philip in 1676 and the close of the war caused the remaining Native American lands in present-day Marion to pass into the hands of the English by right of conquest as the spoils of war.

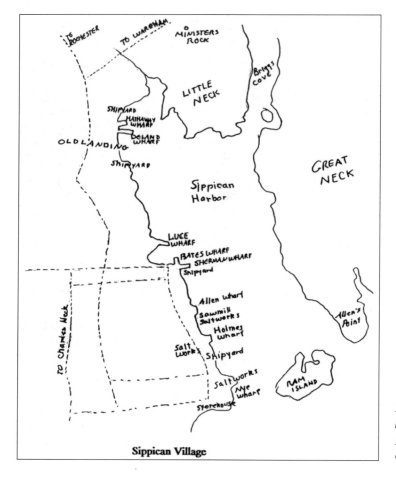

Sippican Village

By 1680, Rochester had 14 tenants at Little Neck and Great Neck.

PERMANENT SETTLEMENT: 1675–1775

The first permanent settlement in Sippican began in 1678 when 29 Pilgrim families left Plymouth and settled in the Little Neck area of present-day Marion at the head of Sippican Harbor. The Pilgrims found the area rich in shellfish (including oysters, clams, scallops, and quahogs) and renamed the area Rochester after the town in Kent County, England (also known for its oysters) from which many of them had come. Rochester-Towne included present-day Rochester, Marion, Mattapoisett, and western Wareham. Thus, the Pilgrims settled where the main Sippican Indian settlement had been located during the 1640s. It was here that the first church services took place, using as a pulpit the same rock that the Native Americans had used in their own ceremonies (renamed Minister's Rock by the Pilgrims).

In 1679, the Rochester proprietors assigned Thomas Hinckley, William Paybody, Joseph Warain, Samuel White, and Joseph Lathrop to survey the Sippican grant, and 16 proprietors each received a house lot consisting of 20 acres and a woodland lot consisting of 40 acres. The Rochester Proprietary was formed, and on July 22, 1679, it purchased from the colony for 200 pounds (to be applied to the debt incurred by King Philip's War) a township grant of all the lands on Buzzards Bay between Dartmouth, Middleboro, and Agawam. The whole territory was often referred to as the "lands of Sippican."

Settlements then began to spread out to Great Neck along the shores of the Weweantic River, Charles Neck (today called Converse Point), Great Hill, and Aucoot Cove. It was allowed that those that "mislike" their home lots at Sippican might take up home lots in any "unlayed out lands from Charles his meadow and the long swamp to Sippican River." The first and second home lots on Great Neck and two lots of the best of the woodland were also set aside for the minister and the ministry. Those who drew home lots at Sippican were the minister, the church, Elizabeth Ellis, James Clarke, William Clarke, Samuel Briggs, Seth Pope, William Paybody, Joseph Burge, Benjamin Foster, Benjamin Bartlett, Kenelm Winslow, Ralph Powel, Joseph Dunham, Thomas Clark, and Aaron Barlow. These 16 shares were situated at Little Neck at the head of Sippican Harbor and at Great Neck in East Marion.

By 1680, Rochester-Towne had 14 tenants. The settlement on Little Neck expanded along Sippican Harbor, and villages were established at Old Landing on the west side of Little Neck and at the Lower Landing, or Wharf Village, which eventually evolved into Marion's center. The original settlement area at Minister's Rock in Little Neck was eventually forsaken, and the original Little Neck church building was converted into a corncrib around 1703. A new meetinghouse was built in 1714 along with additional shipyards, wharves, supply shops, and homes for seafaring families. At the Old Landing village, Marion's first two stone wharves were built in 1708 and two shipyards were established, along with supporting stores such as ship chandleries. From the very beginning, Sippican in Rochester-Towne depended on the sea for its livelihood and survival.

By the middle of the eighteenth century, Old Landing and Wharf Village had a prosperous industrial and commercial economy based on salt manufacturing, fishing, shipbuilding, whaling, and trading with other colonies as well as with Europe, Africa, and the West Indies. Saltworks, wharves, and docks were built to support fishing, whaling, shipbuilding, and salt manufacturing as these industries grew.

FEDERAL PERIOD: 1775–1830

War broke out with England in 1775, and until that time Marion residents had remained sympathetic to their British homeland. Marion had a defenseless coast and was reliant on its water-based industries; however, war with the British interrupted and crippled the town's necessary activities. Marion's lucrative maritime trade was blockaded by the British, who had the largest and most powerful navy in the world. The village of Sippican was never a battleground, but many local residents fought alongside other American Patriots. Elnathan Haskell of Rochester-Towne became a major in the Continental Army and was one of Washington's aides. His portrait is part of the painting by John Trumbull entitled *The Surrender of General Burgoyne at Saratoga, 16 October 1777*, which now hangs in the U.S. Capitol Rotunda.

John Trumbull's 1821 painting of the British surrender at Saratoga that ended the Revolutionary War shows Elnathan Haskell of Rochester, who was an aide to George Washington. Haskell is seventh from right behind the cannon. British Lieutenant General John Burgoyne is left of center handing his sword to American Major General Horatio Gates.

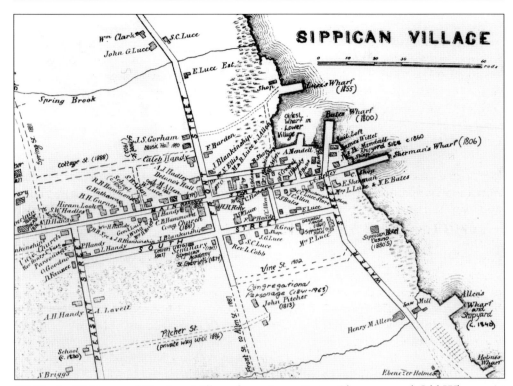

Walling's 1855 map of Sippican Village shows Luce, Bates, Sherman, and Old Wharves in the lower village.

The devastation of the maritime economy of Sippican Village was severe enough that many industries did not fully recover until the early nineteenth century. Following the Peace of Paris in 1783, which ended the Revolutionary War, men returned to rebuild the destroyed economy of their hometowns. Shipyards and saltworks were put back into operation. A dozen or more of the 60 ships that sailed out of Sippican went in search of whales. Fishing was taken up once again, and coastal trade, especially with Southern states such as South Carolina that could provide oak timbers for the shipbuilding industry back home, began in earnest. Eventually progress was made, and the first half of the nineteenth century became the most prosperous period for Sippican's maritime industries, which thrived. Sea captains, shipbuilders, and salt makers bought land and built their homes in present-day Marion, and the money poured in as residential development became concentrated in Old Landing and Wharf Village.

At least three wharves were built at the foot of Main Street (Luce's, Bates's, and Sherman's), and from these, vessels ventured out to fish, whale, and trade. Bird Island Lighthouse was also built around this time. By 1812, coasting sloops of 75 to 120 tons burden were being built in the Wing Shipyard at the shores of the Weweantic River on the north side of Great Neck. A saltworks was built along this

17

same shore. By 1816, the shipyards of Sippican Village and Mattapoisett owned "60 sail" and employed 215 men. The lumber for shipbuilding, as well as for homebuilding, came from the lumber mills on the Sippican River, today's Rocky Knook area. By 1795, Marion's two main centers of maritime development were located at Old Landing and at the end of Main Street in the Lower Village.

After 1800, salt production became the town's number-one business in revenue, and by 1806, more salt was manufactured in Sippican than in any other community in Rochester township. Saltworks spread from the Lower Village to north of Old Landing, and Marion was exporting 20,000 bushels during its peak years before the hurricane of 1815 destroyed much of the industry, including the Delano saltworks on the Weweantic River.

EARLY INDUSTRIAL PERIOD: 1830–1870

The three areas that comprised Rochester-Towne (Rochester, Sippican, and Mattapoisett) gradually grew apart because of their divergent interests. In 1841, the name Sippican appeared for the first time on the U.S. commissioner's list of whaling voyages, replacing the name Rochester. Finally, Sippican officially broke away from Rochester and was incorporated in 1852 as Marion. The coasting sea captains had become enthralled with South Carolina's Revolutionary War hero Francis Marion and decided to name their town after him, believing that "Marion" had a nicer ring to it when hailed over the water than did "Sippican."

South Carolina Revolutionary War hero Francis Marion is portrayed in John Blake White's painting General Marion Inviting a British Officer to Share His Meal.

The brig Herald, *commanded by Rufus Gray, was built in 1846 in Rochester, Massachusetts (Sippican). This painting was made by William Hare, who was born in England c. 1815 and died in Baltimore in 1865. He was a portrait and marine painter from 1842 until his death. (Courtesy Kendall Whaling Museum.)*

With the introduction of the railroad in 1852, vacationers discovered Marion and the pleasant afternoon sea breezes that waft in off the ocean. The New York, New Haven & Hartford Railroad brought vacationers from New York, while the New Bedford & Onset Street Railway line linked New Bedford with Marion and Cape Cod. In 1860, a large wooden hotel called the Marion House was built on Great Hill. Additionally, Joseph Snow Luce inherited an old farmhouse called the Hiller Farmhouse and renovated it in 1864 to become the Bay View House, another summer hotel. Summer visitors would stay at these two hotels or rent houses and often, after becoming smitten with Marion, they began to build summer estates. Some also purchased and refurbished the homes of the former maritime elite.

When the Civil War began in 1861, a number of Marion ships were called into service. Several old local whaling ships were purchased by the government and deliberately sunk in December 1861 as part of the Stone Fleet, which blockaded the harbor at Charleston, South Carolina. In 1862, the Marion-built *Altamaha* was seized and burned by a Confederate naval patrol.

After the Civil War ended in 1865, Marion's maritime industries declined. The foremost cause was the discovery of oil in Pennsylvania, which replaced the demand for whale oil. Salt was also discovered in Pennsylvania and that, along with the invention of the canning process for preserving food, ended the need for large quantities of salt. In addition, Marion's shallow harbor was unable to accommodate the larger ships being built in Boston and New York, and railroads began to replace the coastal shipping trade. In 1865, only three Marion shipyards were still in operation. By 1867, town records indicated that only 26 captains and 46 sailors resided in Marion. Finally, the abandonment of the whaling fleet in Arctic ice in 1871 effectively ended Marion's major involvement in the whaling industry.

LATE INDUSTRIAL PERIOD: 1870–1915

Wealthy summer visitors began coming to Marion via the railroads in the late nineteenth century, bringing with them an intellectual and creative renaissance to the small coastal town. Known as the "Gilded Age" of Marion because of the visiting writers, artists, actors, politicians, and philanthropists, it was also a time of cultural and material wealth that helped lead to the rebirth of the town. The summer visitors who came in droves from 1880 to 1915 chose Marion for its natural beauty and for its harbor, which provided excellent opportunities for fishing and sailing. Guests also enjoyed the predictable afternoon sea breezes that blew in off Buzzards Bay.

Friends join Grover Cleveland (right) on his Marion porch during the summer of 1887. From left are Reverend Percy Brown, Reverend Richard Fuller, and Frances Cleveland.

Chatting in Richard Watson Gilder's Old Stone Studio in 1888 are, from left to right, the mother of Mrs. Grover Cleveland; actor Joseph Jefferson and his wife; Richard Watson Gilder; Mrs. Grover Cleveland; and Mrs. Gilder. The large stone fireplace was designed by Stanford White, partner in the architectural firm McKim, Mead, and White.

Two summer visitors in particular gave the town a tremendous impetus for its rebirth as a summer community: Richard Watson Gilder and President Grover Cleveland.

President Cleveland referred to Marion as "the most beautiful little town in the United States and the little Naples of America." Cleveland was the only American President to win two non-consecutive terms in the White House and the only one to get married while in the White House. In 1889, he lost his bid for a second term to Harrison, even though he had a plurality of 96,000 votes. During the four years between his two terms, Cleveland summered in Marion and went fishing with Joe Jefferson and Clarke Davis (Richard Harding Davis's father). The President went back to his law practice after he lost the election in 1889 and was so employed until he won the next presidential election and was inaugurated again in 1893. Cleveland continued to summer in Marion and wrote from the old Kelly farmhouse (present-day 46 Water Street) on June 9, 1890, while looking out over Little Island:

> I started the fishing branch of the firm's business today and am glad to report that the season promises well. I found here a feeling of depression in the trade and on every side there seemed to be the gravest apprehension for the future. I determined to test the condition and am entirely satisfied that if the industry is properly cared for and prosecuted with zeal, industry and intelligence, satisfactory returns may be

21

confidently relied upon. I caught 25 fish with my own rod and reel, averaging larger than any fish we caught last summer, about equally divided in number between bass and tautog.

When John Luce, the owner of the Bay View House, died in 1882, his hotel was purchased by Charles Ripley, who expanded the resort and called it the Sippican Hotel. He also built a casino across the street on the water. During the 1890s and early 1900s, members of Marion's summer community built beautiful vacation homes along Marion's shoreline. Many of these were built in the Shingle style, which was popular in summer communities on the ocean. In 1909, the Stone family purchased Great Hill and the Marion House. They tore down the old hotel and built a large stone home out of hayden stone that was completed in 1911.

MODERN PERIOD: 1915–2002

Marion has continued to develop as a summer resort community, and because of its well-protected harbor, private beaches, and sparkling outer bay, the community has grown from a sleepy seaside village to the residential and retirement area known today. Marion began with a tiny but stalwart population that made a living from saltworks, shipbuilding, and whaling. It then became the home of many retired sea captains, and soon summer visitors began to come for the beauty of the village and the bay, for the fishing, and for the sailing. These guests loved the smell of tidal marshes and the bracing quality of the sea air. They built their magnificent homes on the shore along with their clubs and their docks, becoming largely responsible for the later economic growth of Marion.

Tabor Academy was reorganized in 1916 and permitted to break Mrs. Taber's codicil to her will requiring free admission. The institution was then allowed to charge tuition beginning in 1928 and only boys were allowed to board at the school. In 1936, Tabor Academy and the Town of Marion exchanged parcels of land and Tabor relocated its facility to the shore. The town acquired 10 acres upland, while Tabor acquired 3 acres on the bay. Tabor, now a coed independent school with approximately 500 students, continues to capitalize on its seaside location.

In 1914, the Marconi Wireless Telegraph Company came to Marion to establish an important station that was in use through World War II. In 1958, the Sippican Corporation was established in Marion and today provides jobs for 450 employees making probes for oceanographic research. The town is also the home of a variety of small businesses and light industry.

Marion has also retained its resort-like atmosphere, and the Beverly Yacht Club has continued its active role in teaching sailing and sponsoring yacht races, including the Marion-to-Bermuda Cruising Yacht Race. It also hosts many national regattas and other sailing competitions. Sailors participating in these events and programs learn self-reliance, independence, and sportsmanship, characteristics that are manifested today by the residents who make up the proud community of Marion.

2. Wharves, Shipyards, and the Shipbuilding Industry

Since roads in the new country were rough and poor, transportation was slow and laborious. The sea offered a much quicker and easier means of communication with the outside world, and the rivers and coasts also served as important routes for transportation.

In the Rochester area, many of the new settlers originally hailed from Kent in England, a community noted for its shipbuilding, and they began to develop that same industry in their new home in Sippican, first for transportation and then for trade. A life at sea offered adventure and an escape from the dull routine for the community's farm boys, many of whom began careers at sea at the age of 14, and almost every house in the village could boast a sea captain in the family. In the beginning, the coasting trade used relatively small vessels such as ketches and shallops and transported products from Sippican up and down the Atlantic seaboard. As the shipbuilding industry in Sippican grew, larger vessels were built and some ventured offshore in pursuit of whales.

Vessels were built in Sippican as early as the 1740s, but Marion's shipbuilding industry was limited due to the shallowness of both Sippican Harbor and the Weweantic River. Thus, Marion's industry specialized in smaller coastal trading and whaling ships of moderate draft. John and Butler Wing were the major shipbuilders of the late eighteenth century in Sippican, and their Wing Shipyard, located on the Weweantic River, was best known for producing coasting ships of 75 to 120 tons burden to carry products such as Marion salt to Southern ports. The coasting vessels would then return north with white oak for the shipbuilding industry at home, as well as cotton and rice for Europe. During the nineteenth century, William Clarke, Edward Sherman, and John Delano were the leading local shipbuilders, and the 1816 census lists 215 men employed by the Sippican and Mattapoisett shipyards with "60 sail" owned by the two ports. By 1867, Marion boasted 67 master-mariners, or captains, and 23 sailors.

Early ships were built on a cooperative plan, and a vessel, once produced, was the joint property of a number of individuals who had contributed to the enterprise. The mechanical work was contributed by some, others furnished timber, ironwork, sails, and rigging, while some contributed money. Oak was used for the ships' hulls and pine for the spars. Malleable fittings and anchors

The first two wharves in Marion were built at Old Landing in 1708: Hathaway's Wharf and Delano's Wharf.

were forged from Marion bog iron, and Marion fields grew the flax for sails, rope, and linseed oil.

Wilson Barstow, who died in his nineties in 1891, said that "vessels were built here as early as 1740 or 1750, sloops and small schooners. There was no science, they were built by sight of the eye and good judgment." There was no drafting and no models. Shipbuilders laid the keel, affixed the stem and stern and the midship frame or rib set-up, then they added a few more ribs between the midship and the ends of the vessel. They affixed the ribbands, or thin strips of boards from the bow to the stern, and the remaining frames were made to fit the lines produced by the ribbands, according to Barstow.

But sometimes this inexact method did not work out very well. One sloop from the period was nicknamed "Bowline" because she was so crooked. The old 448-ton whaler *Trident*, built in 1828, was so much out of true that she carried 150 barrels more oil on one side of the keel than the other. She was described as being "logy" (slow) on one tack, but sailed "like the mischief" (very fast) on the other.

In the late eighteenth and early nineteenth centuries, a sloop or schooner would be constructed in Sippican in the winter and then sold to Nantucket or Old Dartmouth (now called New Bedford). The purchase money was then divided among those who contributed to the boat's construction and played a significant role in the increasing prosperity of the town of Rochester. Sometimes, a vessel was not sold but rather was sailed for profit by the joint owners. Before the Revolutionary War, a sloop named *Planter* was built and run as a freighter from Rochester. The town also produced small whaling vessels, and one sloop named *Defiance* began its voyages from Rochester in 1771.

The first two wharves in Marion—Hathaway's Wharf and Delano's Wharf— were built at Old Landing in 1708. The owners received a fee of "one shilling in money for every boat's load of white caeder brought on or carried off," and many successful boatyards were built at these two wharves. The next wharves to be built in Marion were located in Lower, or Wharf Village. Old Wharf, as its name suggests, was the oldest wharf in the Lower Village. Bates's Wharf (later called Union Wharf) was built in 1800. Sherman's Wharf (later called Central Wharf, and then Long Wharf) was built in 1806 and became the base for a large shipyard.

Captain Henry Allen's Wharf and Shipyard was engaged in building whalers on the harbor off Water Street in front of Allen's home at today's 60 Water Street. Holmes's Wharf and Shipyard was located farther down Water Street (across from present-day Holmes Street), and still farther down Water Street was Nye's Wharf, built in 1839 by Barnabus B. Nye and John B. Blankenship. Nye's Wharf was a very profitable business that serviced whalers and other sailing ships but was eventually abandoned when Marion's maritime industries failed. By 1893, George A. Nickerson bought the adjoining property and used the old wharf for boating, swimming, and fishing.

Alice Austin Ryder's 1934 history of Marion entitled *Lands of Sippican* provides an account of the ships that were built in Marion. Ryder reports that in 1912 80-year-old Charles Henry Delano, the town clerk of Marion, compiled a list of the ships that were built and launched before 1860 by William Clark at the Island Ship Yard, now the town park and wharf near the present-day Barden's Boat Yard. Clark lived on Front Street in a home eventually purchased by Richard Watson Gilder as a summer home.

Delano's list included the following ships: the brig *Herald*, the ship *John Denham*, and the schooners *Angel*, *C.J. Jones*, *J. Vail*, *Hopeton*, *Home*, and *Roswell King*. Delano also recorded that at Sherman's Wharf (the present-day location of the Beverly Yacht Club and the former summer home of Admiral Andrew Harwood), Edward Sherman had built the schooners *Ocean Queen*, *John Frazier*, and *Edward Franklin*. At the shipyard at Delano's Wharf at Old Landing, John Delano had built the *Broadfield*, *Richard M. Demill*, *Abby Elizabeth*, and *Oliver Cromwell*. Just north of Delano's Wharf, at the shipyard at Hathaway's Wharf, Charles Delano recalled that a sloop called the *Georgia* and a schooner called the *Cotton Planter* had been built.

Other records provide accounts of some of the early shipbuilding activities in Marion. In an old sheepskin book from Sherman's Wharf, there is an entry that reads, "Sept. 23, 1805—Silas Briggs and George B. Nye Reckoned and settled all

Book Accounts Except the two Last Settlements of the Sloope *Salley Run* and maid an Even Balance as witness our Hands." Another entry in June 1806 states, "Stephen Luce, Dr. to drawing 267 feet of pine timber for the Sloop *Earl* $6.47. to drawing 55 ft. of Oak timber—$2.06." In July 1807, a long page of items paid to Stephen Barden appears in relation to the sloop *Reformation* and "To an order I gave Seth Haskel on *Little James*."

Despite these and other partial records, there has never been a complete list of ships built in the shipyards of present-day Marion. Not only have most of the old records been completely lost, but most ships were listed as having been built in Rochester, which at one time included both present-day Mattapoisett and present-day Marion. Fortunately, in 1940, the Work Projects Administration compiled a book entitled *Ship Registers of New Bedford, Massachusetts* as part of the National Archives Project. It listed all ships that passed through the New Bedford Customs District, which regulated "the collection of duties imposed by law on the tonnage of ships or vessels and on goods, wares and merchandise imported into the United States" beginning in 1796. These careful records included, among other things, when and where a vessel was built.

Until 1852, when Marion broke away from Rochester and was incorporated as a separate town, all ships built in Marion were listed in the *Ships Register* as having been built in Rochester. Since Rochester included both Marion (Sippican Harbor) and Mattapoisett, one cannot distinguish from the *Ships Register* which harbor built a Rochester-built vessel.

Fortunately, Mattapoisett historian Charles S. Mendell Jr. delivered a paper at a meeting of the Old Dartmouth Historical Society on July 15, 1937, entitled "Shipbuilders of Mattapoisett," in which he culled from the records of shipyards in Mattapoisett (before the 1938 Hurricane destroyed all records) a list of ships built at those shipyards. Thus, it may be concluded that any vessel listed in the *Ships Register* as built in Rochester and not included on Mendell's list was built in a Marion shipyard. The following records detail the 52 ships built in Marion from 1759 to 1854:

1759

   Susa (sloop). Registered June 10, 1799, New Bedford. 74.77 tons. Master: Richard Wood. Owners: Joseph Whelden and Robert Bennett.

1782

   Delight (sloop). Registered September 23, 1801, Hartford, Connecticut. 31 tons and 92 feet; length, 49 feet; breadth 15 feet, 3 inches; depth, 5 feet. Master: Isaac Mason. Owners: Isaac Mason and Francis Brown. One deck, square stern, no galleries, no figurehead. Previously registered at New Bedford on July 15, 1801.

1790

   Surprise (sloop). Registered December 14, 1799, New Bedford. 42.35 tons. Owners: Benjamin Spooner and John Congdon.

This c. 1955 photo shows three wharves built in Lower, or Wharf Village, c. 1800 that remain today in Marion's inner harbor: (from left to right) Sherman's (later Central, then Long Wharf), Bates's (later Union Wharf), and Luce's (now Island Wharf). Beverly Yacht Club is to the left of Sherman's Wharf.

1792

Anna (sloop). Registered November 27, 1799, New Bedford. 62.25 tons. Master: Shubael Hawes. Owners: John Bennett and Benjamin Lincoln.

1797

Union (sloop). Registered June 25, 1802, Rochester. 61 tons and 78 feet; length, 60 feet; breadth, 18 feet, 2 inches; depth, 6 feet, 7 inches. Master: Sanford Taber. Owners: Wilson Barstow, Prince Snow, James Snow, Rebecca Snow, Thomas Clark, Joseph Meiggs, Ephraim Dexter, and Reuben Dexter. One deck, square stern, no galleries, billethead. Previously registered at New Bedford on November 28, 1800.

1798

Susan (sloop). Registered June 14, 1802, Rochester. 62 tons and 70 feet; length, 59 feet, 8 inches; breadth, 18 feet, 4 inches; depth, 6 feet, 8 inches. Master: Eleazer Hathaway Jr. Owners: Wilson Barstow, Gideon Barstow Jr., Jonathan Moore Jr., and Prince Hammond. One deck, square stern, no galleries, no figurehead. Previously registered at New Bedford on November 23, 1798.

1800

Laurel (sloop). Registered April 6, 1808, Rochester. 55 and 27/95 tons; length, 57 feet, 6 inches; breadth, 17 feet, 5 inches; depth, 6 feet, 5 inches. Master: Elephat Loring. Owner: William Moore. One deck, square stern, no galleries, no figurehead. Previously registered at Baltimore, Maryland, on March 5, 1808.

1802

Brutus (brig). Registered December 18, 1801, Rochester. 127 tons and 14 feet; length, 68 feet, 3 inches; breadth, 21 feet; depth, 10 feet, 4 inches. Master: Aseph Price. Owners: Aseph Price, Nathaniel Hammond, Caleb Meiggs, Joseph Meiggs, Jesse Hammond, John Atsett, Benjamin Hammond, Luke Dexter, Samuel Dexter, Andrew Southard, Seth Ames, and Wilson Barstow. One deck, two masts, square stern, no galleries, no figurehead.

Vulture (schooner). Registered December 15, 1802, Rochester. 86 tons and 75 feet; length, 63 feet; breadth, 20 feet; depth, 8 feet, 1 inch. Master: Stephen Hammond. Owners: Stephen Hammond, Nathan Willis, and George B. Nye. One deck, two masts, square stern, no galleries, no head. Previously registered at New Bedford on November 16, 1801.

Rambler (schooner). Registered July 13, 1803, Rochester. 79 and 4/95 tons; length, 63 feet; breadth, 19 feet, 6 inches; depth, 7 feet, 6 inches. Master: Theophilus Pease. Owners: Theophilus Pitcher, Stephen Luce, George B. Nye, Rowland Luce, John Keen, John Clap, Seth Hiller, Elisha Wing, and Stephen Hammond. One deck, two masts, square stern, no galleries, no figurehead. Previously registered at Savannah, Georgia, on May 5, 1803.

Rover (sloop). Registered March 28, 1807, Harwich. 37 and 45/95 tons; length, 50 feet, 5 inches. Owners: Benjamin Nickerson (mariner) and Linzy Nickerson. One deck, square stern, no galleries, no figurehead. Previously registered at New Bedford on April 1, 1805.

Sally (schooner). Registered December 3, 1802, Rochester. 90 and 30/95 tons; length, 64 feet, 6 inches; breadth, 19 feet, 6 inches; depth, 8 feet, 4 inches. Master: Eleazer Hathaway Jr. Owners: Thomas Cook Jr.(New Bedford) and Nathan Willis (Rochester). One deck, two masts, square stern, no galleries, no figurehead. Stephen Luce, surveyor.

1803

Derby (sloop). Registered December 25, 1819, New Bedford. 47 and 39/95 tons; length, 52 feet; breadth, 17 feet, 5 inches; depth 5 feet, 3 inches. Master: Henry Wady. Owner: Shadrack Standish. One deck, square stern, no galleries, no figurehead. Previously registered at New Bedford on November 8, 1819.

Patty (brig). Registered January 3, 1804, Rochester. 129 tons; length, 70 feet; breadth, 21 feet, 6 inches; depth, 10 feet. Master: Nathan Clark. Owners: George B. Nye, Rowland Luce, Stephen Luce, and Nathan Clark. One deck, two masts, square stern, no galleries, no head. Calvin Delano, surveyor.

1804

Cato (ship). Registered July 6, 1804, Rochester. 265 tons; length, 89 feet, 3 inches; breadth, 26 feet, 2 inches; depth, 13 feet, 1 inch. Master: James Snow. Owners: Wilson Barstow, Jonathan Moores, Moores Rogers, Gideon Barstow Jr., Benjamin Barstow, and Caleb Dexter (Rochester); Gideon Howland, Andrew Swain, and Jethro Allen (New Bedford). Two decks, three masts, square stern, no galleries, no figurehead. Name of master carpenter not available. Calvin Delano, surveyor.

Danube (brig). Registered January 26, 1805, New Bedford. 193 and 66/95 tons; length, 78 feet, 10 inches; breadth, 23 feet, 10 inches; depth, 11 feet, 11 inches. Master: Gilbert Howland. Owners: Gilbert Howland and John H. Howland. Two decks, two masts, square stern, no galleries, no figurehead. Rounsevel Spooner, surveyor.

These are examples of the various types of whaling vessels built in Marion.

Laura (schooner). Registered June 12, 1806, Rochester. 98 and 75/95 tons; length, 67 feet; breadth, 19 feet, 8 inches; depth, 8 feet, 2 inches. Master: Stephen Burgess. Owners: Stephen Burgess (Harwich), Butler Wing and Samuel Haskell (Rochester), David Burgess (Dartmouth), and Robert Bennett (New Bedford). One deck, two masts, square stern, no galleries, no figurehead. Previously registered at Norfolk and Portsmouth, Virginia, on February 8, 1806.

Minerva (ship). Registered February 1, 1805, Rochester. 349 and 14/95 tons; length, 89 feet; breadth, 25 feet, 4 inches; depth, 12 feet, 8 inches. Master: Stephen Hammond. Owners: Stephen Hammond and Nathan Willis (Rochester), Abraham Barker (New York), and Josiah Richmond (Dighton). Two decks, three masts, square stern, no galleries, no figurehead. Stephen Luce, surveyor.

Renown (schooner). Registered March 30, 1808, Rochester. 78 and 11/95 tons; length, 65 feet, 6 inches; breadth, 19 feet, 9 inches; depth, 7 feet. Master: Jabez Delano. Owners: Jabez Delano, Philip Allen, Justus Allen, Cornelius Briggs, John Caswell, Roland Briggs, and Harper Delano. One deck, two masts, square stern, no galleries, no figurehead. Previously registered at Philadelphia, Pennsylvania, on December 10, 1807.

A topsail schooner of the early nineteenth century is engaged in whaling in this drawing by Clifford W. Ashley.

1805

Amazon (brig). Registered December 11, 1805, New Bedford. 214 and 9/95 tons; length, 82 feet, 6 inches; breadth, 24 feet, 6 inches; depth, 12 feet, 3 inches. Master: Thomas Clarke. Owners: John H. Howland, Jonathan Allen, Thomas Clarke, and Prince Allen (New Bedford) and Gideon Barstow Jr. (Rochester). Two decks, two masts, square stern, no galleries, no figurehead. Rounsevel Spooner, surveyor.

1806

Honestas (ship). Registered December 31, 1806, New Bedford. 301 and 25/95 tons; length, 97 feet; breadth, 26 feet, 7 inches; depth 13 feet, 3.5 inches. Master: Nathan Clark. Owners: John H. Howland and Thomas Hazard Jr. (New Bedford) and Gideon Barstow Jr. (Rochester). Two decks, three masts, square stern, no galleries, no figurehead. Rounsevel Spooner, surveyor. Captured in 1813.

Indian Queen (ship). Registered July 7, 1806, Rochester. 339 and 21/95 tons; length, 103 feet, 8 inches; breadth, 27 feet, 2 inches; depth, 13 feet, 7 inches. Master: Stephen Hammond. Owners: Nathan Willis, Stephen Hammond, and Josiah Richmond. Two decks, three masts, square stern, no galleries, no figurehead. Stephen Luce, surveyor.

Sally (schooner). Registered May 29, 1806, New Bedford. 78 and 2/95 tons; length, 60 feet, 2 inches; breadth, 18 feet; depth, 8 feet, 4 inches. Master: Gilbert Howland. Owner: Gilbert Howland. One deck, two masts, square stern, no galleries, alligator head. Rounsevel Spooner, surveyor.

1807

Horizon (ship). Registered May 26, 1809, Rochester. 272 and 86/95 tons; length, 91 feet; breadth, 26 feet, 3 inches; depth, 13 feet, 1.5 inches. Master: William LeBaron. Owner: William LeBaron. Two decks, three masts, square stern, no figurehead. Calvin Delano, surveyor.

Sophia (sloop). Registered July 12, 1810, Rochester. 66 tons; length 62 feet; breadth, 19 feet, 5 inches; depth, 6 feet, 7 inches. Master: Ebenezer Bolles. Owners: Obed Bolles, Ebenezer Bolles, Lot Haskell, John Clap, Levi Gurney, Ebenezer Haskell, Stephen Delano Jr., and Abraham Burgess. One deck, square stern, no galleries, no figurehead. Previously registered at New Bedford on September 8, 1809.

1809

Hermit (sloop). Registered August 18, 1810, New Bedford. 56 and 91/95 tons; length, 56 feet, 1 inch; breadth, 18 feet, 6 inches; depth, 6 feet, 6 inches. Master: Charles Burgess. Owners: Lovi Jenney, John Delano, and John Johnson. One deck, square stern, no galleries, no figurehead. Previously registered at New Bedford on November 11, 1809.

1810

Mercy (sloop). Registered July 24, 1815, Rochester. 63 and 92/95 tons; length, 58 feet; breadth, 20 feet, 1 inch; depth, 6 feet, 6 inches. Master: Savery Boles. Owners: Savory Boles, William Boles, John Clapp, Caleb Dexter, and Obed Boles. One deck, square stern, no galleries, no figurehead. Previously registered at Passamaquoddy on June 22, 1815.

Susan (sloop). Registered May 21, 1811, Sandwich. 39 and 77/95 tons; length, 52 feet, 4 inches; breadth, 17 feet, 6 inches; depth, 5 feet, 2 inches. Master: Abner Ellis. Owners: Abner Ellis, Josiah Ellis, and Josiah Ellis Jr. One deck, square stern, no galleries, no figurehead. Previously registered at New Bedford on May 8, 1810.

Tybee (brig) Registered January 12, 1811, New York. 288 and 40/95 tons; length, 85 feet; breadth, 24 feet, 4 inches; depth, 12 feet, 8 inches. Master: William Thomson. Owners: Nathan Willis and Josiah Richmond (Rochester) and Samuel Bell (New York). One deck, two masts, square stern, no galleries, a billet figurehead. Calvin Delano, surveyor.

1811

Betsey (sloop). Registered August 26, 1815, Rochester. 72 and 21/95 tons; length, 58 feet, 10 inches; breadth, 18 feet, 9 inches; depth, 8 feet, 0.5 inch. Master: Timothy Hiller Jr. Owners: Charles Blankinship and Stephen Hammond (Rochester) and Nathan Willis (Pittsfield). One deck, square stern, no galleries, no figurehead. Previously registered at New Bedford on October 28, 1811.

Caroline (brig). Registered October 10, 1812, Rochester. 52 and 90/95 tons; length, 75 feet; breadth, 22 feet, 3 inches; depth, 10 feet, 7 inches. Master: Timothy Wing. Owners: Carl Church, Timothy Wing, Elisha Ruggles, Alfred Kindrick, John Clapp, George B. Nye, and Seth Haskell. One deck, two masts, square stern, no galleries, no figurehead. Previously registered at New Bedford on October 17, 1811.

Sally (schooner). Registered October 12, 1812, Rochester. 93 and 2/95 tons; length, 63 feet, 2.5 inches; breadth, 20 feet, 3.5 inches; depth, 8 feet, 6.5 inches. Master: Philip Wing. Owners: Philip Wing, Noah Dexter, Benjamin Dexter, Abraham Burgess, Nathaniel Haskell Jr., and Freeman Dean. One deck, two masts, square stern, no figurehead. Previously registered at New York on March 20, 1812.

1812

Baltic Trader (ship). Registered March 14, 1812, Rochester. 380 and 49/95 tons; length, 106 feet, 10.5 inches; breadth, 28 feet, 4.5 inches; depth, 14 feet, 2.25 inches. Master: Andrew Southworth. Owners: Wing Hadley, Nathan Willis, Stephen Hammond, Peleg Tripp, and Josiah Richmond (Rochester) and Abraham Barker (New York). Two decks, three masts, square stern, no galleries, no figurehead. Wing Hadley, master carpenter. Butler Wing, surveyor.

Excellent (brig). Registered June 7, 1852, Mattapoisett. 67 and 78/95 tons; length, 55 feet, 6 inches; breadth, 18 feet, 4 inches; depth, 7 feet, 11 inches. Master: Benjamin Smith. Owners: John T. Atsatt, Lot N. Jones, James Washburn, Philip Atsatt, Roland Howland, Arvin Cannon, Dennis S. Boodry, Rogers L. Barstow, Leonard Robbins, and Elisha Dexter (Rocheser). One deck, two masts, square stern, no galleries, a billethead. Previously registered at Bristol and Warren, Rhode Island, on October 13, 1851.

1814

Harmony (sloop). Registered August 7, 1815, Rochester. 85 and 10/95 tons; length, 63 feet; breadth, 19 feet; depth, 8 feet, 3 inches. Master: Obed Boles. Owners: Obed Boles, Josiah Holmes, David Hiller, Jonathan Hiller, Ebenezer Holmes, David Hall, Caleb Dexter, Edward Shearman, Ephraim Allen, and Ebenezer Boles. One deck, square stern, no galleries, no figurehead. Previously registered at New Bedford on May 4, 1815.

Long Wharf appears here in 1915.

1817

Dolphin (schooner). Registered April 24, 1818, Harwich. 41 and 55/95 tons; length, 52 feet, 9.5 inches; breadth, 16 feet, 10.75 inches; depth, 5 feet, 6 inches. Master: Osborn Snow. Owners: Osborn Snow, David Snow, Isaiah Deane, Josiah Deane, and Elijah Deane. One deck, two masts, square stern, no galleries, no figurehead. Previously registered at New Bedford on April 9, 1817.

1825

China (schooner). Registered September 30, 1825, New Bedford. 96 and 67/95 tons; length, 71 feet, 7 inches; breadth, 21 feet; depth, 7 feet, 5 inches. Master: Melatiah B. Perry. Owners: Melatiah B. Perry (New Bedford), Daniel Perry (Fairhaven), and David Anderson (New York). One deck, two masts, square stern, no galleries, a billethead. Certificate of master carpenter on file. Wilber Southworth, surveyor.

1826

Marmion (schooner). Registered September 3, 1827, Rochester. 99 and 44/95 tons; length, 70 feet, 1 inch; breadth, 21 feet, 5 inches; depth, 7 feet, 8.5 inches. Master: Amos Headley. Owners: Noble E. Bates, Ebenezer Bowls, John Blankinship, Barnabas B. Nye, Jonathan Dexter, Benjamin Delano, Stephen Delano, Elijah Luce, John Pitcher, Peleg S. Pitcher, Stephen C. Luce, James

This drawing of the brig Frances A. Barstow *was made by Clifford W. Ashley.*

Delano, Caleb Handy, Weston Allen, Ebenezer Holmes, Rowland Luce Jr., Joseph Allen, Henry D. Delano, Joseph Handy, Bethuel Dexter, Barnabas Holmes, Jonathan Handy Jr., and Theophilus Pitcher Jr. One deck, two masts, square stern, no galleries, a billethead. Previously registered at New Bedford on December 21, 1826.

1828

Pilot (sloop). Registered July 13, 1831, Yarmouth. 57 and 92/95 tons; length, 56 feet; breadth, 19 feet; depth, 6 feet, 6 inches. Master: Joseph Baker. Owner: Joseph Baker. One deck, square stern, no galleries, a billethead. Previously registered at New Bedford on August 31, 1829.

1831

Virginia (sloop). Registered September 15, 1834, St. Mary's, Georgia. 59 and 17/95 tons; length, 60 feet, 2.5 inches; breadth, 20 feet; depth, 5 feet, 10 inches. Master: Francis Chavalier. Owners: Francis Chavalier. One deck, square stern, no galleries, a billethead. Previously registered at New Bedford on October 1, 1833.

1832

Edward Franklin (schooner). Registered June 11, 1836, Rochester. 118 and 37/95 tons; length, 70 feet, 7 inches; breadth, 21 feet, 7 inches; depth, 9 feet, 0.5 inch. Master: Leonard Berry. Owners: Edward Shearman, Job Blankinship, and Paddock Bates. One deck, two masts, square stern, no galleries, a billethead. Previously registered at Darien, Connecticut, on March 15, 1836.

1834

Florida (schooner). Registered June 14, 1837, New Bedford. 74 and 70/95 tons; length, 64 feet, 4 inches; breadth, 19 feet, 8 inches; depth, 6 feet, 10 inches. Master: Benjamin Savory. Owners: Charles H. Warren (New Bedford), William B. Swett (Boston), Timothy Savery Jr. (Wareham), and Thomas Russell (Plymouth). One deck, two masts, square stern, no galleries, a billethead. Previously enrolled at New Bedford on July 21, 1836.

Stranger (schooner). Registered October 22, 1841, Sandwich. 82 and 42/95 tons; length, 63 feet, 4 inches; breadth, 20 feet, 2 inches; depth, 7 feet, 7 inches. Master: Henry L. Blackwell. Owner: Henry Blackwell. One deck, two masts, square stern, no galleries, a billethead. Altered in description. Previously enrolled at New Bedford on September 14, 1840. Francis Howard, surveyor.

1835

Meridian (brig). Registered August 24, 1840, Wareham. 72 and 89/95 tons; length, 61 feet, 2 inches; breadth, 20 feet, 2 inches; depth, 7 feet. Master: Thomas Derrick. Owners: Moses L.F. Tobey, Josiah H. Hall, John Washburn,

Ira Maham, Daniel Weston, Joshua B. Tobey, Joshua Gibbs III, Ozier Howard, and James Holmes (Wareham), Ansel White (Fairhaven), Benjamin Ellis, Jesse Murdock, and John Savery (Carver), Ellis Griffith, Thomas Washburn, and Solomon Washburn (Middleborough). One deck, two masts, square stern, no galleries, a billethead. Previously enrolled at New Bedford on September 27, 1839.

1836

Altamaha (schooner). Registered June 10, 1839, Rochester. 119 and 37/95 tons; length, 60 feet, 9 inches; breadth, 22 feet, 6 inches; depth, 8 feet, 4 inches. Master: Nathan Briggs. Owners: Walton N. Ellis, Henry M. Allen, Elisha Luce, Stephen C. Luce, John Clapp, George Ellis, and Rowland Luce. One deck, two masts, square stern, no galleries, a billethead. Previously enrolled at New Bedford on June 6, 1838.

1837

Roswell King (schooner). Registered June 27, 1851, Sippican. 134 and 61/95 tons; length, 74 feet; breadth, 23 feet, 7 inches; depth, 9 feet, 0.75 inch. Master: George Look. Owners: William C. Mendell, Peleg Blankenship, and Ebenezer Holmes (Rochester) and John Butler and Pierce Butler (Philadelphia). One deck, two masts, square stern, no galleries, a billethead. Previously enrolled at New Bedford on July 26, 1848.

Washington (brig). Registered January 22, 1828, Plymouth. 168 and 83/95 tons; length, 78 feet, 4 inches; breadth, 21 feet, 8 inches; depth, 11 feet, 4 inches. Master: John Burgiss. Owners: Charles Bramhall, John Burgiss, Isaac L. Hedge, Thomas Hedge, Henry Jackson, Henry Weston, John Harlow II, and William Harlow. One deck, two masts, square stern, no galleries, a billethead. Previously enrolled at New Bedford on December 18, 1827.

1846

Herald (brig). Registered July 7, 1849, Sippican. 174 and 38/95 tons; length, 73 feet, 2 inches; breadth, 24 feet, 3 inches; depth, 9 feet, 4 inches. Master: Russell Gray. Owners: Stephen C. Luce, Frederick B. Bolles, Henry M. Allen, Ebenezer Holmes, John G. Luce, Samuel W. Luce, and William Taylor (Rochester) and Seth Russell (New Bedford). One deck, two masts, square stern, no galleries, a billethead. Previously enrolled at New York on April 5, 1849.

1849

Hopeton (schooner). Registered May 21, 1849, Sippican. 145 and 21/95 tons; length, 81 feet, 8 inches; breadth, 23 feet, 3 inches; depth, 8 feet, 9 inches. Master: Jabez Delano. Owners: Samuel W. Luce, William Clark, Henry M. Allen, Walton N. Ellis, Peleg Blankenship, and Frederick B. Bolles (Rochester).

One deck, two masts, square stern, no galleries, a billethead. Previously registered at New Bedford on June 27, 1848.

J. Vail (schooner). Registered May 15, 1849, Sippican. 164 and 61/95 tons; length, 87 feet, 1.5 inches; breadth, 23 feet, 4 inches; depth, 9 feet, 2 inches. Master: David Jenney. Owners: George Delano (Rochester). One deck, two masts, square stern, no galleries, a billethead. Previously enrolled at New Bedford on September 9, 1848.

1853

Emily (bark). Registered October 7, 1853, New Bedford. 294 and 20/95 tons; length, 107 feet, 9 inches; breadth, 26 feet, 2 inches; depth, 11 feet, 1.4 inches. Master: George H. Keen. Owners: Simpson Hart, William H. Taylor, Zeno Kelley, Joseph Clark, George A. Bourne, William G. Parker, George Tappan, Joseph G. Dean, James D. Driggs, John Baylies and Timothy Ingraham of J. Baylies & Co., George G. Gifford, Horace Humphrey, Nathan Chase, John W. Nickerson, Bela C. Perry, Nathan Lewis and Leonard Crowell of N. Lewis & Co., Edward Cannon and Richard Curtis of Edward Cannon & Co. (New Bedford), Stephen Delano, and George H. Keen (Sippican). One deck, three masts, square stern, no galleries, a billethead. Certificate of master carpenter on file. Charles C. Allen, surveyor.

A c. 1886 coasting schooner is the subject of this drawing by Albert Bigelow.

1854

Abby Elizabeth (brig). Registered May 24, 1856, New Bedford. 194 and 20/95 tons; length, 95 feet; breadth, 26 feet; depth, 8 feet, 11.25 inches. Master: Abraham Phinney. Owners: Joseph Clark, Simpson Hart, James Durfee, William Beetle, and Charles S. Randall (New Bedford), Joshua B. Tobey (Wareham), Moses H. Swift (Marion), and Heman Phinney and Abraham Phinney (Sandwich). One deck, two masts, square stern, no galleries, a billethead. Previously registered at New York on January 20, 1855.

Although shipbuilding ended in Marion in 1854 after the *Abby Elizabeth* was built and before the Civil War began, whalers continued to sail from Sippican Harbor in Marion until 1880, when the *Admiral Blake* sailed on her last whaling voyage. Because Marion's harbor was too shallow to build the larger whalers necessary for longer voyages, shipbuilding moved on to other ports with deeper water.

The schooner Admiral Blake *is pictured here at dock.*

3. WHALING

Native Americans and the early Pilgrims used whales chiefly for food. The whaling industry developed into a large commercial industry because of the discovery in the early seventeenth century that whale oil could be burned in lamps for light. As early as 875 A.D., whale fishing is documented along the French coast, but this may have been only the cutting up of stranded whales. Up to the sixteenth century, the Norwegians, French, Icelandic, and English were engaged in whale fishery; thus, the Pilgrims who settled in New England were at least familiar with its methods and products. As early as 1641, Captain John Smith, sailing along the coast of New England, sighted large numbers of whales and pursued them.

The recorded history of the American whale fishery began with the colonies; however, Native Americans were skilled in capturing whales long before that time. There is mention in early colonial records of whale meat used as food and a reference by a Plymouth historian to the boldness shown by Native Americans who attacked whales from open canoes, killing them with crude spears when the creatures came to the surface to breathe. More often, however, they would wait for a whale to wash ashore, whereupon they would cut the flesh into pieces and share it with neighboring tribes. During the time that Native Americans lived in Sippican, whales were plentiful along the coast and in the deeper water offshore. The English settlers in Marion likely increased their take of beached or "drift" whales by pursuing them in Buzzards Bay with small craft. They would then beat the water with oars in front of a pod of whales to drive any panicked ones onto the shore.

In 1639, Massachusetts passed an act to encourage whale fishery, providing that vessels engaged in whaling were exempt from all duties and taxes for a period of seven years. In addition, those employed in whaling were excused from military service during the whaling season. Sloops of 12 to 30 tons, fitted for cruises of a few weeks, soon began to be used in whaling efforts. This organized and deliberate pursuit of offshore whales began in the colonies during the third quarter of the seventeenth century. These sloops carried enough casks to hold the blubber of one whale. The sloops generally sailed in pairs and divided their catch equally. They also typically carried two boats. One was held in reserve in case the

Hervey E. Luce   Thomas Nye Jr.

The Luce and Nye families were among the many who captained whale ships out of Marion.

one lowered for whales became damaged. The sloops returned with the whale blubber, and it was cut up and "tried out" (boiled) in tryworks on the shore.

During the first half of the eighteenth century, whale fishery underwent a steady development in both technique and scale. As the shore population of whales was depleted, larger sloops, schooners, and brigs were used and the act of "trying out" was done on board, making longer and more profitable voyages possible. At first, ships of this sort were 60 to 70 tons and carried about 14 men in the crew. The tool kit available to the whaler was also improved to include harpoons, lances, whale-line, cutting-spades, and other articles.

At this time, there were two important advances in technology that profoundly altered the scope and shape of American whaling: the installation of tryworks on shipboard and the utilization of spermaceti—a waxy substance found in the head of sperm whales—to manufacture candles. The onboard tryworks, iron pots set in a brick furnace, permitted the rendering of oil from blubber without returning to shore. The oil was then stored in barrels without the worry of blubber deterioration.

The use of sperm whale oil in candle manufacture had important effects as well. While coastal whaling yielded right whales, the more desirable sperm whales were found offshore in deep water. The oil they produced was lighter, purer, and usually brought in three times more money than other types of whale oil; therefore, the potential for financial gain significantly increased the incentives to engage in sperm whaling. This led to longer voyages and the development of more seaworthy craft.

Whaleships were constructed to carry a large amount of special gear and equipment not required by clippers and other merchant ships, such as heavy brick tryworks and iron trypots; cooling tanks; casks for oil; spare whaleboats; and whalecraft and gear for capturing, cutting-in, and trying-out whale blubber; as well as general supplies for voyages that could last from three to five years. Whalers averaged between 250 and 400 tons, were approximately 100 feet on deck, and were bulky. While the ratio of beam to length on clipper ships averaged one to six, that same ratio on whaleships was approximately one to four.

Above the water line, whaleships also differed greatly from any other type of merchant vessel. On the port side, three whaleboats were slung from wooden davits about 10 feet in height, another boat was carried at the starboard quarter, and most of the larger ships also carried a starboard bow boat. The space amidships on the starboard side had a section of the bulwarks (gangway) that could be removed when cutting-in the blubber from whales. The tryworks, erected on deck forward of the fore hatch, consisted of a brick furnace containing two iron trypots, each having a capacity of about 250 gallons. The strength of these ships was their seaworthiness and their ability to carry a full cargo of oil together with the mass of necessary whaling gear and food supplies. Whaleships were the most solidly built ships afloat in their time.

The period from 1750 to 1784 was perhaps the most eventful for the American whaling industry. Ancillary support industries such as rope making, coopering, blacksmithing, and carpentry sprang up, and by the onset of the Revolutionary War, whaling-related activities had surpassed all other colonial maritime industries. By 1775, a total of 304 whaling vessels sailed annually from Massachusetts ports with an annual take of 45,000 barrels of sperm oil, 8,500 barrels of whale oil, and 75,000 pounds of whale bone.

But the Revolutionary War (1775–1783) caused a setback in whaling. British blockades forced the cessation of most maritime activities, and British frigates often seized American whaleships, forcing the crews into the king's service. Despite this, whaling revived quite rapidly at the end of the war and ships were soon fitted for longer and more far-reaching voyages. Sloops and schooners were converted into larger brigs and ships of 200 to 500 tons, requiring crews of 30 men or more. New Bedford soon raced ahead, leading Nantucket in both number of vessels and tonnage, because Nantucket's harbor was shallower.

Marion's participation in whaling began in earnest around 1784, and by 1786, four Marion-based vessels were engaged in the trade, many carrying familiar local names such as Blankinship, Hammond, Bates, Luce, and Nye. In 1770, a Rochester-owned whaling schooner named *Desire*, owned by Ebenezer White, set out with Captain Nye. Other Rochester whaleships of the era included *Henry*,

Gold Hunter, James Lopez, Napoleon, and *Julian.* As early as 1790, these larger vessels began traveling to the Pacific Ocean. Archilus Hammond of Rochester is credited with killing the first sperm whale in the Pacific Ocean on the *Amelia,* which sailed out of Nantucket and around Cape Horn to the Pacific.

Other vessels soon ventured around the Horn, including *President, John Adams, Sally, Magnolia, George, Hero, Ontario, Orion, Spartan, Swift, Zone, Omega,* and *Meridian.* Not every voyage was profitable. In 1796, the whaling ship *Harmony* under Captain George Blankinship left from Rochester, ran upon a whale off the coast of Brazil, was stove, and sunk. The crew was saved, but the vessel and cargo were lost.

The War of 1812 and the British practice of impressing crews of American ships again caused serious damage to the whaling industry. But after the peace treaty was signed in 1814, whaling recovered quickly and once again moved forward. The three decades following 1820 were considered "the golden age of whaling," when individual voyages often lasted three to four years.

In present-day Marion (then still part of Rochester), whalers left for long voyages taking with them local men and boys. Although many returned with their barrels full of oil, many were wrecked along the way. Sometimes whalers returned having lost part of their crew. If a ship returned to Sherman's or Luce's Wharf with its flag flying at the top of the masthead, Marion villagers knew that all was well on board. If the flag was flown at half mast, someone aboard had died.

Whaling reached its peak in 1857, four years before the start of the Civil War, with 329 whaleships sailing out of New Bedford. In 1858, Marion's industrial census listed 25 whaling ships as either Marion or Mattapoisett owned. During the height of whaling, 23 Sippican-built whalers made nearly 100 voyages from the wharves of Marion.

The Civil War, however, severely damaged the industry and helped bring about its doom. Rebel cruisers destroyed 50 whaleships. Many others were sold and still others transferred to the merchant service. The U.S. government purchased 40 whalers for the "Stone Fleet," which was sunk off the Savannah and Charleston harbors to prevent the entrance of blockade-runners. These whalers left New Bedford Harbor in 1861 filled with stones to ensure they would sink. It is possible that three of the whalers in the fleet—*Amazon, Cossack,* and *Herald*—were built in Sippican; however, only the *Cossack* had the same rigging as ships built in Marion. The U.S. government purchased the *Amazon* for $3,670, the *Cossack* for $3,200, and the *Herald* for $4,000. In addition to the Civil War's damaging effect on the industry, the discovery of mineral oil and petroleum reduced the demand for sperm and whale oil.

In 1871, the Arctic fleet was virtually destroyed when it became ice-locked. The abandonment of the *Awashonks* and *Gayhead* in Arctic ice that year nearly ended Marion's involvement in the whaling industry. By 1884, the town's fleet consisted of only the *Admiral Blake,* Marion's last whaler. The last New England–based whaler was the *Charles W. Morgan,* which was abandoned in 1924 at the port of New London.

In 1931, Theodore Tripp, the last of the old whalemen of Sippican, told of his first voyage on May 16, 1861, when he sailed out of Sippican Harbor on the *Altamaha*:

> You know, I'd never seen a whale until I was in the boat pullin' an' one of them ugly critters came right up along side of me. I jumped and Jarvis sez—you know Jarvis Blankinship, he's the mate I told you weighed me and said I didn't weigh more'n a dried codfish—well, Jarvis, he hollered, "What's the matter, Tripp? What you 'fraid of?" You know a green horn flopped sometimes and he didn't want me keeling over there. "Next time he comes up that way, Tripp," Jarvis sez, "You spit in his eye! Don't you be afraid till you see my gills whiten." When the line you're sittin' in flies out an' you have to bail to keep it from smokin', I tell you there's more truth than po'try in the sayin' "A dead whale or a stove boat." The ugly critter a'rarin' and a'tarin' and the *Altamaha* a mile away. Yes, it was the *Altamaha*, 1861. Course the whale boat is big—twenty-five, thirty feet; oars, fourteen, fifteen feet long—and it has took the boys half a day to coil the line in the boat so there's no kinks in it. When the critter is struck and dashing ahead, with the boat flying through the foam, there's some says you better not change your quid nor breathe or you'll upset her. A fightin' whale can pull out a powerful lot of line—miles—and all

This engraving of a whaling scene was made for the Colonial Society of Massachusetts from an original lithograph.

the harpoons you can stick in him! When you git him you are sometimes six miles from the ship, and then alongside! And sharks! The water's full of 'em! And then cuttin' in! Blubber peeled off in strips, and try her out like your Ma used to try out lard when the hog is killed in the fall. An' then the oil in the cooler, and run through to the casks. Used to use leather hose. Then it's clean up the ship. Some captains throw the tryworks overboard, and everybody is set to paintin'. If the ship's full, we sing the old *Altamaha* song. "It's when you see those New Bedford girls/Good by, fare you well; good by, fare you well/With their bright blue eyes and flowing curls/Hurrah my boys, we're homeward bound."

Many of the local boys that went out on whalers moved up the ranks, becoming mates of schooners in the Liverpool and Southern trade, then on to American clipper ships.

As the young men of the villages rose to become mates and then captains—40, 50, 100 of them—they became men of intense individuality and figures of great distinction. As mates they learned to know and discipline men. As captains, they learned to transact business.

Melville wrote in *Moby Dick* that "a sea captain is a man who has been led to think untraditionally and independently."

Several boats from different whaleships attack whales.

These boy captains, who earned their titles often by 21 years of age and who sometimes retired at 35, dealt in their small sea kingdoms with perilous situations in strange far-off waters. Only men of a strong type could face the challenges of not only the baffling winds of the oceans, but also the baffling moods of the suave traders in the ports. It was sometimes a respectful opinion, sometimes an instant decision, sometimes a grave silence that was imperative to make a voyage successful.

At the beginning of the nineteenth century, all the men of Rochester were captains, ship builders, or saltmakers. By 1809, every family in town was represented by a least one captain and sometimes two or three in distant waters with the following names:

Adams
Allen (Albert, Joseph, James,
   Ephraim)
Barden
Bates (Joseph, Sylvester,
   George, Roland, Albert)
Blackmer
Blankinship (James, George,
   Job, Seth, Peleg)
Bolles (William, Frederick,
   Savory, Obed)
Briggs (Paul, Hallett,
   Nathaniel)
Church
Clapp
Clark (James, Henry, Elisha,
   Lemuel, Lem Jr.)
Cleghorn
Coleman
Crandon
Davis
Delano (Stephen, Franklin)
Fuller
Hammond (Alfred Elnathan,
   Nathaniel, Gideon, Nathan,
   Stephen, Jabez, Israel)

Hiller
Jenney
Keen
Look
Lovell
Luce
Norton
Nye
Pierce
Pope
Rogers
Ruggles
Ryder
Sherman
Snow
Sprague
Swift
Taber
Weeks
White (Resolved, Resolved Jr.)
Wing (Quaker Captains John,
   Resolved, Timothy, David,
   Jedidiah, Stephen, Samuel,
   Clifton, Paul)
Winslow

Alexander Starbuck's 1877 *The History of the American Whale Fishery* is the classic text about whaling prior to 1876. The United States Commissioner of Fish and Fisheries commissioned Starbuck to prepare a historical sketch of the whaling industry in the United States and to append to it, so far as was practical, a record of every voyage that had been undertaken. So, Starbuck examined newspapers covering a 170-year period, as well as books, documents, and other records of the ports of Boston and New Bedford and compiled a list of whaling vessels and their voyages from 1784 to 1876. Starbuck acknowledged that the list might be incomplete; however, it was the best that was available and represented an enormous undertaking.

Starbuck stated that "[f]ew interests have exerted a more marked influence upon the history of the United States than that of the fisheries." In addition to whaling's importance as a commercial venture, he said it also attracted whalemen who were a "hardy, daring, and indefatigable race of seamen, such as scarcely any other pursuit could have trained." He also noted that "[i]nto the field opened by them flowed the trade of the civilized world." Starbuck believed that the development of the whaling industry in the United States, "from the period when a few boats first practiced it along the coast to the time when it employed a fleet of seven hundred stanch ships and fifteen thousand hardy seamen," was a very interesting chapter in our national history.

The book contains tables showing the returns of whaling vessels sailing from American ports beginning in the year 1784. From that time until 1852, present-day Marion was part of Rochester, which also included present-day Mattapoisett. Accordingly, during that period, Starbuck's tables just listed Rochester as the sailing port.

It is not known which vessels sailed out of Sippican Harbor (Marion) and which sailed out of Mattapoisett Harbor. After 1840, Marion vessels are listed under Sippican as the sailing port. Starting in 1866, Marion is listed as the home port. The following is a summary of the whaling voyages out of Marion:

1816
   Sally (schooner), Captain Smith, last reported in July with 50 sperm.

1820
   Orion (brig), Captain Luce, whaling ground Cape Verde Islands, departed June 25, last reported with 150 sperm.

1822
   Pocahontas (brig), Captain Johnson, whaling ground Atlantic, departed October, last reported with 35 sperm.

1826
   Magnolia (schooner), 98 tons, Captain Randall, whaling ground Atlantic, returned August 23, 1827, sperm oil 150 barrels, whale oil 15 barrels.

1827
   Magnolia (schooner), Captain Randall, whaling ground Atlantic, departed October, returned June 2, 1828, last reported with 300 sperm.
   Sophronia (schooner), whaling ground Atlantic, last reported with 120 sperm.

These examples of scrimshaw, the folk art of American whalemen, are in the collection of the Nantucket Historical Society.

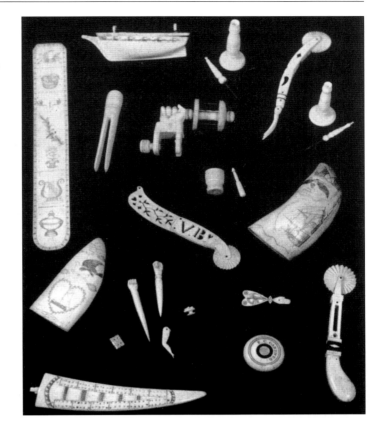

1828

Magnolia (schooner), 98 tons, Captain George Lewis, whaling ground West Indies, departed June and December 15, returned August 1829, sperm oil 95 barrels, whale oil 40 barrels.

Sophronia (schooner), Captain Daggett, whaling ground Atlantic, departed May 18, last reported with 190 sperm.

1829

Magnolia (schooner), Captain Lewis, whaling ground Atlantic, departed January, reported in May with 40 sperm.

Sophronia (schooner), Captain Daggett, whaling ground Atlantic, departed April 30, September 3, returned August and September 17, sperm oil 50 barrels, reported 90 sperm.

1830

Franklin (bark), 252 tons, Captain Nathaniel C. Cary, whaling ground Brazil, departed July 3, returned May 21, 1831, whale oil 1,750 barrels.

Lexington (schooner), Captain Daggett, whaling ground Atlantic, returned

September 24, sperm oil 70 barrels.
Sophronia (schooner), lost at sea August 17.

1831

Dryade (bark), Captain Nathaniel C. Carey, whaling ground South Atlantic, Departed July 13, returned April 24, 1832, whale oil 1,200 barrels.
Franklin (bark), 251 tons, Captain Priam P. Brock, whaling ground South Atlantic, departed July 20, returned April 23, 1832, whale oil 1,400 barrels.
Lexington (schooner), Captain Daggett, whaling ground Atlantic, returned July 15, sperm oil 20 barrels.
Laurel (schooner), Captain Taber, whaling ground Atlantic, returned August 4, sperm oil 90 barrels, whale oil 40 barrels.

1832

Dryade (bark), 348 tons, Captain George H. Richmond, whaling ground South Atlantic, departed May 3, returned March 22, 1833, whale oil 1,300 barrels.
Franklin (bark), Captain Priam P. Brock, whaling ground South Atlantic, departed May 31, returned May 12, 1833, whale oil 700 barrels—Captain Brock and his boat's crew lost while fast to a whale, September 23, 1832.

A 250-gallon trypot is pictured here before being re-set on the deck of a whaleship.

1833

Dryade (bark), Captain Joseph R. Taber, whaling ground Pacific Ocean, departed May 29, returned April 21, 1834, sperm oil 350 barrels, whale oil 850 barrels.

Franklin (bark), Captain Calvin C. Adams, whaling ground South Atlantic, departed June 27, returned April 1835, sperm oil 200 barrels, whale oil 1,300 barrels.

Laurel (schooner), Captain Mayhew, whaling ground "Western Islands," departed April 2, returned November 12, sperm oil 275 barrels.

Shylock (ship), 277 tons, Captain Clement Hammond, whaling ground Indian Ocean, returned June 11, 1834, whale oil 650 barrels.

1834

Dryade (bark), 263 tons, Captain Joseph R. Taber, whaling ground Atlantic, departed July 3, returned December 14, 1835, sperm oil 140 barrels, whale oil 1,630 barrels.

Laurel (schooner), Captain Mayhew, whaling ground Atlantic, returned November 5, sperm oil 290 barrels.

Shylock (ship), Captain Clement Hammond, whaling ground Atlantic, departed July 15, returned May 24, 1835, sperm oil 200 barrels, whale oil 900 barrels, whale bone 6,000 pounds.

1835

Laurel (schooner), Captain Mayhew, whaling ground Cape de Verdes, returned November 27, sperm oil 300 barrels, whale oil 15 barrels, probably sailed twice, also returned June 7, 110 sperm.

Orion (brig), Captain Snow, whaling ground Atlantic, departed April 22, returned July 1, sperm oil 275 barrels.

Shylock (ship), 277 tons, Captain Hallett Swift, whaling ground South Atlantic, departed July 13.

1836

Annawan (brig), 148 tons, Captain Snow, Captain Hammond, whaling ground Atlantic, departed April 8 and returned November 20, departed December 16 and returned June 19, 1837, sperm oil 250 barrels and 178 barrels, whale oil 50 barrels and 20 barrels.

Caduceus (brig), 109 tons, Captain Southworth, whaling ground Atlantic, departed April 30—supposed to have foundered at sea and all hands lost.

Dryade (bark), 263 tons, Captain Smalley, sperm oil 28 barrels, whale oil 1,813 barrels.

Gideon Barstow (ship), 379 tons, Captain Severance, whaling ground Cape de Verdes, departed June 15, returned March 25, 1838, sperm oil 158 barrels, whale oil 2,527 barrels.

Laurel (schooner), Captain Luce, whaling ground Cape de Verdes, departed

April 24, returned December 5, sperm oil 60 barrels.

Mattapoisett (ship), Captain Southworth, whaling ground Cape de Verdes, departed April 23, reported with 140 sperm.

Orion (brig), Captain Daggett, whaling ground Cape de Verdes, departed April 8, returned October 14, sperm oil 400 barrels.

Sarah (ship), Captain Mayhew, whaling ground Cape de Verdes, departed May 4, reported with 250 sperm in September.

1837

Annawan (brig), 148 tons, Captain Snow, whaling ground Atlantic, departed July 20, returned June 27, 1838, sperm oil 308 barrels, whale oil 35 barrels.

Lagrange (brig), 170 tons, Captain Daggett, whaling ground Atlantic, departed April, returned March 17, 1838, sperm oil 240 barrels, whale oil 660 barrels.

Le Barron (brig), 170 tons, Captain Rogers, whaling ground Atlantic, departed July 29, returned September 5, 1838, sperm oil 601 barrels.

Mattapoisett (brig), 150 tons, Captain Southworth, whaling ground Atlantic, departed March 25, returned March 22, 1838, sperm oil 483 barrels, whale oil 25 barrels.

Orion (brig), 99 tons, Captain Wing, whaling ground Atlantic, departed April 21, returned October 5, sperm oil 80 barrels, whale oil 15 barrels.

Shylock (ship), 278 tons, Captain Taber, whaling ground South Atlantic, departed July 2, returned December 6, 1838, sperm oil 41 barrels, whale oil 2,444 barrels.

Sarah (brig), 171 tons, Captain Mayhew, whaling ground Atlantic, departed March 25, returned June 7, 1838, sperm oil 416 barrels, whale oil 25 barrels.

1838

Annawan (brig), 148 tons, Captain Charles Bates, whaling ground Atlantic, departed July—lost at sea in a gale, March 1839, captain, first and second mates, and 12 men lost.

Dryade (bark), 263 tons, Captain Smalley, whaling ground Indian Ocean, departed July 3, returned October 23, 1839, sperm oil 242 barrels, whale oil 1,350 barrels.

Gideon Barstow (ship), 379 tons, Captain Cary, whaling ground Indian Ocean, departed June 20—lost at Cocos Islands, March 1839.

Lagrange (brig), 170 tons, Captain Daggett, whaling ground Atlantic, departed April 30, returned May 10, 1839, sperm oil 431 barrels, whale oil 5 barrels.

Le Barron (brig), 170 tons, Captain Rogers, whaling ground South Atlantic, departed October 20, returned November 7, 1839, sperm oil 646 barrels.

Mattapoisett (brig), 150 tons, Captain Southworth, whaling ground Atlantic, departed April 3, returned June 4, 1839, sperm oil 220 barrels.

Orion (brig), 99 tons, Captain Purrington, whaling ground Atlantic, departed September 13, returned May 27, 1839, sperm oil 120 barrels.

Sarah (brig), 171 tons, Captain Purrington, whaling ground Atlantic, departed

The trypots are set and then bricked in aboard a whaleship.

July 22, returned May 16, 1839, sperm oil 563 barrels.
Solon (brig), 129 tons, Captain Hammond, whaling ground Atlantic, departed June 6, returned April 16, 1839, sperm oil 440 barrels.

1839

Chase (brig), 153 tons, Captain Mayhew, whaling ground Atlantic, departed August 21, returned October 23, 1840, sperm oil 430 barrels—abandoned at sea, 1841.

Lagrange (brig), 170 tons, Captain Riddell, whaling ground Atlantic, departed June 30, returned June 21, 1840, sperm oil 52 barrels.

Mattapoisett (brig), 150 tons, Captain Southworth, whaling ground Atlantic, departed July 14, returned December 14, 1840, sperm oil 300 barrels.

Orion (brig), 99 tons, Captain Snow, whaling ground Atlantic, departed June 23—lost at Puerto Rico, March 22, 1840.

Pearl (brig), 157 tons, Captain Purrington, whaling ground Atlantic, departed July 4, returned June 24, 1840, sperm oil 130 barrels, whale oil 30 barrels.

Richard Henry (bark), 173 tons, Captain Ellis, whaling ground Atlantic, departed August 17, returned August 18, 1840, sperm oil 300 barrels—Captain Ellis was killed by a whale on July 24, 1840.

Shylock (ship), 278 tons, Captain Taber, whaling ground New Zealand, departed May 26—lost at Fiji Islands, 1840.

Pictured above is the deck of a whaler.

Sarah (brig), 171 tons, Captain Purrington, whaling ground Atlantic, departed July 7, returned July 13, 1840, sperm oil 500 barrels.

Solon (brig), 129 tons, Captain Wing, whaling ground Atlantic, departed May 17, returned June 2, 1840, sperm oil 200 barrels.

Two Sisters (brig), 122 tons, Captain Hammond, whaling ground Atlantic, departed July 30, returned March 27, 1840, sperm oil 500 barrels, bought from Boston 1839.

Volant (bark), 210 tons, Captain Hammond, whaling ground South Atlantic, departed October 18, sperm oil 120 barrels, whale oil 200 barrels, condemned at St. Helena, February 1841.

Willis (brig), 164 tons, Captain Boodry, whaling ground Atlantic, departed June 16, returned August 28, 1840, sperm oil 475 barrels.

1840

Cossack (bark), 256 tons, Captain Delano, whaling ground Indian Ocean, departed July 9, returned May 10, 1843, sperm oil 350 barrels, whale oil 1,356 barrels, whale bone 11,600 pounds.

Dryade (bark), 263 tons, Captain Rogers, whaling ground Indian Ocean, departed April 13, returned June 17, 1842, sperm oil 725 barrels, whale oil 95 barrels.

Lagrange (brig), 170 tons, Captain Daggett, whaling ground Atlantic, departed September, returned May 9, 1841, sperm oil 600 barrels.

Le Barron (brig), 170 tons, Captain Cushing, whaling ground South Atlantic, departed April 2, returned November 2, 1841, sperm oil 350 barrels.

Pearl (brig), 157 tons, Captain Blankenship, whaling ground Atlantic, departed August 20, returned October 15, 1841, sperm oil 200 barrels—lost a boat's crew to a whale, 1841.

Richard Henry (brig), 134 tons, Captain Dexter, whaling ground Atlantic, departed September 15, returned September 29, 1841, sperm oil 70 barrels.

Sarah (brig), 171 tons, Captain Purrington, whaling ground Atlantic, departed October. 10, returned Apr. 17, 1841, sperm oil 624 barrels.

Solon (brig), 129 tons, Captain Wing, whaling ground Atlantic, departed July 30, returned October 17, 1841, sperm oil 220 barrels.

Two Sisters (brig), 122 tons, Captain Bolles, whaling ground Atlantic, departed May 11, returned June 7, 1841, sperm oil 30 barrels.

Willis (brig), 164 tons, Captain Boodry, whaling ground Atlantic, departed October 4, returned January 1, 1842, sperm oil 260 barrels.

Popmunnett (brig), 184 tons, Captain Flanders, whaling ground South Atlantic, departed May 11, returned October 20, 1841, sperm oil 400 barrels.

Quito (brig), 140 tons, Captain Flanders, whaling ground South Atlantic, departed June 1, returned November 3, 1841, sperm oil 350 barrels.

Solon (brig), 129 tons, Captain Wing, whaling ground South Atlantic, departed July 30, returned September 1842, sperm oil 40 barrels, whale oil 20 barrels.

1841

Drymo (bark), 262 tons, Captain Hammond, whaling ground Pacific Ocean, departed August 5, returned May 21, 1844, sperm oil 600 barrels, bought from Boston 1841, sold to Fairhaven 1844.

Hecla (bark), 207 tons, Captain Crapo, whaling ground Indian Ocean, departed August 16, returned March 1845, sperm oil 900 barrels, bought from New York 1841.

Two Sisters (brig), 122 tons, Captain Bolles, whaling ground Atlantic, departed July 24.

1842

Pearl (bark), 157 tons, Captain Blankenship, whaling ground Pacific Ocean, departed January 12—lost in Japan August 11, 1843, six of her crew lost with her.

Popmunnet (bark), 184 tons, Captain Flanders, whaling ground Atlantic, departed February 20, returned September 23, 1843, sperm oil 350 barrels, whale oil 60 barrels.

Quito (brig), 140 tons, Captain Chase, whaling ground Atlantic, departed May

17, returned October 1842, sperm oil 270 barrels, whale oil 30 barrels.

Solon (brig), 129 tons, Captain Brightman, whaling ground Atlantic, departed October 26, returned November 1843, sperm oil 250 barrels, sold to Mattapoisett 1844.

1843

Cossack (bark), 256 tons, Captain Delano, whaling ground "northwest coast," departed October 24, returned May 21, 1846, sperm oil 80 barrels, whale oil 1,620 barrels, whale bone 14,000 pounds.

Popmunnet (bark), 184 tons, Captain Flanders, whaling ground Indian Ocean, departed December 2, returned July 3, 1845, sperm oil 170 barrels, whale oil 550 barrels, whale bone 3, 000 pounds.

Quito (brig), 140 tons, Captain Chase, whaling ground Atlantic, departed January 9, returned September 21, 1845, sperm oil 280 barrels, whale oil 40 barrels.

1844

Quito (brig), 140 tons, Captain Chase, whaling ground Atlantic, departed January 9, returned September 21, 1845, sperm oil 280 barrels, whale oil 40 barrels. [Note: Although this listing is identical to the listing in 1843, this entry is repeated for it is listed in both 1843 and 1844 by Starbuck.]

1845

Hecla (bark), 207 tons, Captain Hedge, whaling ground Indian Ocean, departed September 26, returned November 10, 1848, sperm oil 450 barrels.

Juno (brig), 123 tons, Captain Bates, whaling ground Atlantic, departed June 18, returned August 21, 1846, sperm oil 300 barrels, withdrawn 1847.

Popmunnet (bark), 184 tons, Captain Tilton, whaling ground Atlantic and Indian Oceans, departed August 22, returned September 10, 1847, sperm oil 300 barrels, sold to Fairhaven 1847—First Mate Lumbert and one man drowned 1846.

1846

Cossack (bark), 256 tons, Captain Dexter, whaling ground Pacific Ocean, departed September 29, returned June 26, 1850, sperm oil 50 barrels, whale oil 1,500 barrels, whale bone 9,000 pounds, sold to New Bedford 1850.

Quito (brig), 140 tons, Captain Chase, whaling ground Atlantic, departed June 14, returned November 11, 1847, sperm oil 270 barrels, whale oil 100 barrels, sold to Nantucket 1848.

1852

Altamaha (schooner), 119 tons, Captain Charles B. Hammond, whaling ground Atlantic, departed July, returned August 15, 1853, sperm oil 60 barrels, whale oil 40 barrels, withdrawn 1853.

These are some of the tools known as whalecraft that were used to hunt whales.

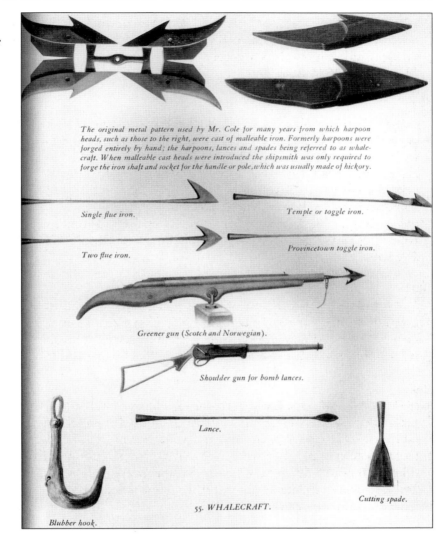

The original metal pattern used by Mr. Cole for many years from which harpoon heads, such as those to the right, were cast of malleable iron. Formerly harpoons were forged entirely by hand; the harpoons, lances and spades being referred to as whalecraft. When malleable cast heads were introduced the shipsmith was only required to forge the iron shaft and socket for the handle or pole, which was usually made of hickory.

Single flue iron.

Temple or toggle iron.

Two flue iron.

Provincetown toggle iron.

Greener gun (Scotch and Norwegian).

Shoulder gun for bomb lances.

Lance.

Cutting spade.

55. WHALECRAFT.

Blubber hook.

1853

   Admiral Blake (schooner), 120 tons, Captain Benjamin B. Handy, whaling ground Atlantic, departed May 20, returned October 5, 1853, sperm oil 140 barrels, whale oil 6 barrels.

1854

   Admiral Blake (schooner), 120 tons, Captain Benjamin B. Handy, whaling ground Atlantic, departed May 12, returned September 8, 1854, sperm oil 156 barrels, whale oil 10 barrels, value of cargo $11,000.
   Altamaha (schooner), 119 tons, Captain Charles Hammond, whaling ground Atlantic, departed May 12, returned November 14, sperm oil 40 barrels.

Captain William Hathaway lifts a harpoon on the deck of the whaleship Admiral Blake, *moored in Marion harbor. Hathaway's home was located on Main Street.*

1855

Admiral Blake (schooner), 120 tons, Captain Benjamin B. Handy, whaling ground Atlantic, departed August 25, returned October 31, 1856, sperm oil 23 barrels, withdrawn 1856.

Altamaha (schooner), 119 tons, Captain Consider Fisher, whaling ground Atlantic, departed May 10, returned November 12, sperm oil 207 barrels, whale oil 12 barrels, total 240 sperm, 8 blackfish, worth $13,510.

1856

Admiral Blake (schooner), 120 tons, Captain Jared Blankenship, whaling ground Atlantic, departed May 13, returned September 14, sperm oil 100 barrels, whale oil 32 barrels.

Altamaha (schooner), 119 tons, Captain Fisher, whaling ground Atlantic, departed May 22, returned August 31, 1858, sperm oil 193 barrels, whale oil 150 barrels.

James (schooner), 80 tons, Captain Benjamin B. Handy, whaling ground Atlantic, departed May 20, returned August 31, sperm oil 193 barrels, brought from New Bedford, 1856, total 220 sperm, worth $10,000.

1857

Admiral Blake (schooner), 120 tons, Captain Jared Blankenship, whaling ground Atlantic, departed May 7, returned October 24, sperm oil 135 barrels.

Altamaha (schooner), 119 tons, Captain Fisher, whaling ground Atlantic, departed July 31, returned April 15, 1857, sperm oil 63 barrels, whale oil 53 barrels. [Note: The April 15, 1857 date is as listed in Starbuck.]

Hopeton (brig), 145 tons, Captain Obed Delano, whaling ground Atlantic, departed June 16, returned April 16, 1859, sperm oil 206 barrels, whale oil 37 barrels, formerly a schooner.

1858

Admiral Blake (schooner), 120 tons, Captain Jared Blankenship, whaling ground Atlantic, departed April 29, returned July 13, 1859, sperm oil 34 barrels, whale oil 44 barrels.

Retrieve (schooner), 100 tons, Captain William C. Hathaway, whaling ground Atlantic, departed May 13, returned August 23, sperm oil 148 barrels, whale oil 5 barrels, bought from Gloucester 1858.

1859

Altamaha (schooner), 119 tons, Captain John C. Clark, whaling ground Atlantic, departed June 29, returned July 24, 1860, sperm oil 151 barrels, whale oil 13 barrels.

Hopeton (brig), 145 tons, Captain Otis S. Snow, whaling ground Atlantic, departed June 2, returned August 29, 1860, sperm oil 255 barrels, whale oil 7 barrels.

James (schooner), 80 tons, Captain Benjamin B. Handy, whaling ground Atlantic, departed May 2, returned September 16, sperm oil 163 barrels, whale oil 6 barrels.

Retrieve (schooner), 100 tons, Captain William C. Hathaway, whaling ground Atlantic, departed May 2, returned September 11, sperm oil 53 barrels, whale oil 1 barrel.

Roswell King (schooner), 134 tons, Captain Pardon Tripp, whaling ground Atlantic, departed April 26, returned August 19, 1860, sperm oil 83 barrels, whale oil 40 barrels.

1860

Admiral Blake (schooner), 120 tons, Captain William C. Hathaway, whaling ground Atlantic, departed April 6, returned September 20, sperm oil 182 barrels, whale oil 2 barrels.

Hopeton (brig), 145 tons, Captain Edwin A. Perry, whaling ground Atlantic, departed October 9, returned November 25, 1861, sperm oil 140 barrels, whale oil 10 barrels, sold for merchant service 1862.

James (schooner), 80 tons, Captain Benjamin B. Handy, whaling ground Atlantic, departed April 30, returned August 29, sperm oil 103 barrels.

The 1906 painting Lowering for a Whale *by Clifford W. Ashley for Harper's Magazine depicts a whaleboat crew preparing to give chase.*

Retrieve (schooner), 100 tons, Captain Zenas F. Eldridge, whaling ground Atlantic, departed April 30, returned September 6, sperm oil 118 barrels.

1861
Admiral Blake (schooner), 120 tons, Captain William C. Hathaway, whaling ground Atlantic, departed May 9, returned September 27, sperm oil 135 barrels.
Altamaha (schooner), 119 tons, Captain Benjamin B. Handy, whaling ground Atlantic, departed May 21—burned at sea by Confederates. [Note: Starbuck writes, "Burned at sea by the rebel cruiser."]
James (schooner), 80 tons, Captain Allen D. Rider, whaling ground Atlantic, departed May 16, returned August 29, sperm oil 125 barrels, whale oil 4 barrels.
Retrieve (schooner), 100 tons, Captain Zenas T. Eldridge, whaling ground Atlantic, departed May 16, condemned at Fayal 1861.

1862
Admiral Blake (schooner), 120 tons, Captain William C. Hathaway, whaling ground Atlantic, departed May 12, returned October 18, sperm oil 10 barrels, whale oil 5 barrels.

Altamaha (schooner), 119 tons, Captain Rufus Gray, whaling ground Atlantic, departed May 12—captured and burned by the CSS *Alabama* 1862.

Emerald (schooner), 101 tons, Captain Zenas F. Eldridge, whaling ground Atlantic, departed May 20, returned October 21, sperm oil 35 barrels, whale oil 5 barrels, bought from Fairhaven 1862.

Hopeton (brig), 145 tons, Captain Benjamin B. Handy, whaling ground Atlantic, departed May 20, returned October 18, sperm oil 138 barrels, withdrawn 1862.

James (schooner), 80 tons, Captain Allen D. Ryder, whaling ground Atlantic, departed May 14, returned September 6, sperm oil 62 barrels, whale oil 7 barrels.

1863

Admiral Blake (schooner), 120 tons, Captain William C. Hathaway, whaling ground Atlantic, departed May 14, returned October 9, sperm oil 105 barrels, whale oil 8 barrels.

Emerald (schooner), 101 tons, Captain Zenas F. Eldridge, whaling ground Atlantic, departed May 23, returned October 17, sperm oil 115 barrels, bought from Fairhaven 1862.

James (schooner), 80 tons, Captain George H. Keen, whaling ground Atlantic, departed May 9, returned August 27, sperm oil 47 barrels, whale oil 15 barrels, withdrawn 1863—lost on Fortune Island February 11, 1864, loaded with salt.

When a whale is sighted, the whaleboats set off under sail in pursuit.

This detail from an early painting by Raleigh shows a whaler about to strike.

Sunbeam (schooner), Captain Benjamin B. Handy, whaling ground Atlantic, departed May 26, returned August 17, sperm oil 45 barrels, whale oil 5 barrels, sold to Plymouth 1863 for mackerel fishing.

1864

Admiral Blake (schooner), 120 tons, Captain William C. Hathaway, whaling ground Atlantic, departed April 29, returned October 12, sperm oil 155 barrels, whale oil 9 barrels.

Emerald (schooner), 101 tons, Captain Zenas F. Eldridge, whaling ground Atlantic, departed May 20—supposed to have foundered at sea with all on board.

1865

Admiral Blake (schooner), 120 tons, Captain William. C. Hathaway and Captain Arthur H. Hammond, whaling ground Atlantic, departed May 2 and returned August 21, departed again December 28 and returned November 4, 1866, sperm oil 285 barrels and 130 barrels, whale oil 2 barrels and 150 barrels.

Herald (brig), 178 tons, Captain John A. Kelley, whaling ground Atlantic, departed October 24, returned August 9, 1866, sperm oil 237 barrels, whale oil 277 barrels, from merchant service,1865.

1866

Herald (brig), 148 tons, Captain John A. Kelley, whaling ground Atlantic, departed December 12, returned September 27, 1868, sperm oil 112 barrels, whale oil 20 barrels, sailed once and returned on account of damage to boats and crew by a whale.

William Wilson (schooner), 92 tons, Captain William C. Hathaway, whaling ground Atlantic, departed May 18, returned August 28, sperm oil 220 barrels, bought from Plymouth 1866.

1867

Admiral Blake (schooner), 84 tons, Captain Arthur H. Hammond, whaling ground Atlantic, departed May 10, returned April 23, 1868, sperm oil 212 barrels, whale oil 32 barrels.

Cohannet (schooner), 83 tons, Captain William. C. Hathaway, whaling ground Atlantic, departed May 13, returned August 14, sperm oil 220 barrels, bought from Boston 1866, value of cargo $13,000.

William Wilson (schooner), 92 tons, Captain Judah Hathaway, whaling ground Atlantic, departed May 10, returned August 28, 1867, sperm oil 185 barrels, whale oil 15 barrels, also 8 pounds of ambergris.

1868

Admiral Blake (schooner), 84 tons, Captain Arthur H. Hammond, whaling ground Atlantic, departed December 3, returned March 13, 1871, whale oil 361 barrels, whale bone 760 pounds, withdrawn for freighting, 1871.

Cohannet (schooner), 83 tons, Captain William C. Hathaway, whaling ground Atlantic, departed May 12, returned October 8, whale oil 7 barrels.

An 1850 drawing by A. Van Beest, R. Swain Gifford, and Benjamin Russell shows the capture of a sperm whale.

A captured whale is brought alongside the whaler to begin cutting-in.

Express (schooner), 80 tons, Captain Handy, managing owner or agent Benjamin B. Handy, whaling ground Atlantic, departed May 20, returned October 12, 1868, sperm oil 17 barrels, whale oil 3 barrels, added 1868.

Graduate (schooner), 58 tons, Captain Allen D. Ryder, whaling ground Atlantic, departed May 12, returned September 21, sperm oil 51 barrels.

Herald (brig), 148 tons, Captain John A. Kelley, whaling ground Atlantic, departed December 18, returned July 27, 1870, sperm oil 270 barrels, withdrawn for merchant service, 1871.

Pocahontas (brig), 200 tons, Captain Micajah C. Fisher, whaling ground Atlantic, departed July 16, bought from New Bedford 1868, condemned at Barbados, October 1870.

William Wilson (schooner), 92 tons, Captain Hathaway, whaling ground Atlantic, departed May 22, returned August 28, sperm oil 162 barrels.

1869

Cohannet (schooner), 83 tons, Captain Obed Delano, whaling ground Atlantic, departed May 18, returned September 19, sperm oil 85 barrels, whale oil 6 barrels.

Express (schooner), 80 tons, Captain Benjamin B. Handy, whaling ground Atlantic, departed May 19, returned June 15, 1870, sperm oil 80 barrels, sold to Provincetown 1871.

Graduate (schooner), 58 tons, Captain Rufus L. Savery, whaling ground Atlantic, departed May 18—lost at sea with five men.

William Wilson (schooner), 92 tons, Captain William C. Hathaway, whaling ground Atlantic, departed May 18, returned October 3, sperm oil 85 barrels.

1870

Cohannet (schooner), 83 tons, Captain James T. Wittet, whaling ground Atlantic, departed May 17, returned September 24, whale oil 8 barrels.

William Wilson (schooner), 92 tons, Captain Hathaway, whaling ground Atlantic, departed May 17, returned September 23, sperm oil 173 barrels.

1871

Cohannet (schooner), 83 tons, Captain Loring Braley, whaling ground Atlantic, departed June 13, returned September 17, sperm oil 150 barrels.

William Wilson (schooner), 92 tons, Captain Hathaway, whaling ground Atlantic, departed May 24, returned September 13, sperm oil 175 barrels.

1872

Admiral Blake (schooner), 84 tons, Captain William. C. Hathaway, whaling ground Atlantic, departed May 22, returned September 29, 1873, sperm oil 24 barrels, whale oil 11 barrels.

Cohannet (schooner), 83 tons, Captain Loring Braley, whaling ground Atlantic, departed January 30 and returned August 31, departed again December 4 and returned September 1873, sperm oil 260 barrels and 158 barrels, whale oil 20 barrels and 2 barrels, sold to Fairhaven, 1874.

William Wilson (schooner), 92 tons, Captain Edward Cluny, whaling ground Atlantic, departed May 27, returned June 15, 1873, sperm oil 22 barrels, whale oil 5 barrels, whale bone 285 pounds.

1874

Admiral Blake (schooner), 84 tons, Captain William C. Hathaway, whaling ground Atlantic, departed May 22 and returned October 6, departed October 27 and returned April 17, 1875, sperm oil 78 barrels and 85 barrels, whale oil 5 barrels.

William Wilson (schooner), 92 tons, Captain Loring Brailey, whaling ground Atlantic, departed June 11 and returned October 9, departed December 2 and returned September 16, 1875, sperm oil 188 barrels and 185 barrels, whale oil 35 barrels.

1875

Admiral Blake (schooner), 84 tons, Captain W.C. Hathaway, whaling ground Atlantic, departed May 26 and returned October 4, sperm oil 195 barrels, whale oil 10 barrels, sailed again in 1875 and returned March 31, 1876, sperm oil 80 barrels, whale oil, 20 barrels.

1876

Admiral Blake (schooner), 84 tons, Captain William C. Hathaway, whaling ground Atlantic, departed May 16, returned October 8, sperm oil 90 barrels, sailed again in December.

William Wilson (schooner), 92 tons, Captain Loring Braley and Captain Charles B. Barstow, whaling ground Atlantic, departed March 27 and returned September 15, departed again November 27 and returned October 1877, reported 60 barrels sperm oil.

In 1959, The Old Dartmouth Historical Society and the Whaling Museum of New Bedford published *Returns of Whaling Vessels Sailing From American Ports: A Continuation of Alexander Starbuck's "History of the American Whale Fishery" 1876–1928.* It was compiled by Reginald B. Hegarty with additions by Philip F. Purrington. The following is a summary of whaling voyages from Marion after 1876:

1876

William Wilson (schooner), 92 tons, Captain Charles B. Barstow, whaling ground Atlantic, departed November 27, returned October 2, 1877, sperm oil 85 barrels, whale oil 125 barrels.

1877

Admiral Blake (schooner), 84 tons, Captain W.C. Hathaway, whaling ground Atlantic, departed November 21, returned September 3, 1878, sperm oil 225 barrels, whale oil 5 barrels.

Benjamin Russell's lithograph View of the Stone Fleet Which Sailed from New Bedford Nov. 16th 1861 *in the New Bedford Whaling Museum shows the bark* Cossack, *which is believed to be from Marion.*

The captains of the Stone Fleet, 1861, appear in this image engraved for the Colonial Society of Massachusetts from a photograph.

William Wilson (schooner), 92 tons, Captain C.B. Barstow, whaling ground Atlantic, departed December 9, returned September 18, 1878, sperm oil 90 barrels.

1878
   Admiral Blake (schooner), 84 tons, Captain W.C. Hathaway, whaling ground Atlantic, departed November 19, returned July 21, 1879, sperm oil 40 barrels.
   William Wilson (schooner), 91 tons, Captain A.H. Hammond, whaling ground Atlantic, departed November 25, returned October 2, 1879, sperm oil 120 barrels.

1880
   Admiral Blake (schooner), 84 tons, Captain W.C. Hathaway, whaling ground Atlantic, departed May 26, returned October 12, sperm oil 170 barrels.
   William Wilson (schooner), 91 tons, Captain A.H. Hammond, whaling ground Atlantic, departed June 24, returned October 2, 1881, sperm oil 160 barrels, whale oil 50 barrels.

Because of Marion's shallow harbor, it never developed as a major whaling port like New Bedford, which was only 11 miles away. However, whaling was very important as a commercial venture in Marion in that it employed so many of its local men and boys. In 1858, 23 Sippican-built whalers made approximately 100 voyages from Marion compared to the 329 whaleships that sailed out of New Bedford, many of which also employed Marion men and boys. Returning captains enjoyed their wealth, building large homes in Old Landing and on Main Street near the harbor of Wharf Village. These hardy seamen contributed to the character and spirit of Marion, still present today.

This is the figure head from the Admiral Blake, *which in 1884 was Marion's last whaler. The vessel cleared $8,000 in two months.*

4. SALT INDUSTRY

For approximately 150 years during the eighteenth and early nineteenth centuries, Sippican's economic mainstay was its salt industry. Residents would boast, "The leading business of Sippican is salt." The product was in great demand during the American Revolution and was used in the preservation and curing of meat and fish. The salt industry was first developed by colonists in response to the British blockade and the imposition of a heavy tax on salt. This early industry illustrates what is often called Yankee ingenuity.

Because of Sippican's coastal situation, its residents were in a prime location to extract salt from the sea. The town's production of salt reached its apex about the time of the War of 1812, when there were more than a score of concerns profitably engaged in it.

The first means of extracting salt from seawater was by boiling the water in kettles. It took 300 gallons of seawater to make a bushel of salt and it also required men, women, and children to continuously cut and burn logs under the big iron pots, which had to be heated all day. This was the method that George Bonum Nye used during his early attempts to manufacture salt in Sippican.

But because it was a slow and tedious process and the forests were fast disappearing, boiling was replaced by solar evaporation. In this method, seawater was pumped upland by windmills through hollowed logs to vats. The saltwater was then moved from vat to vat to be evaporated by the sun, leaving salt deposits at the bottom of the vats.

Wooden roofs swung on cranes were placed over the salt vats at night or when it rained. At one time the western shores along Sippican harbor were lined with windmills.

These salt works consisted of a series of vats between 15 and 18 feet wide, 50 to 60 feet long, and approximately 1 foot deep. The first three vats were called the "water rooms"; the next three, the "pickle rooms"; and the last, the "salt room." Each played its part in the process of evaporation.

The sides of the first water room were covered with vegetation left by the evaporating liquid. In the next two, a thick slime was deposited on the bottom. In the "pickle rooms," lime was precipitated and remained on the bottom when the brine was passed into the "salt room," where the crystals of salt formed. These

The Crocker saltworks were located in Barnstable, Massachusetts.

crystals were then shoveled out and stored in sheds or salt houses to dry. Salt produced by this method was pure, strong, and free from lime.

Because salt was in great demand for the curing of fish, more and more Sippican men became interested in working as part-time salt makers. As soon as fishing vessels arrived in the harbor, the salt-packed fish were washed, loaded into barrels, and wheeled to the "flakes." These were low platforms of slats spread along the upland near the shore. Here, the fish were split, washed again, salted, and laid in the sun to dry. They had to be turned occasionally and, in rainy weather, stacked up and covered with tarpaulins.

The solar evaporation method of salt production started about 1800 when James Clark moved to Sippican from Brewster, on Cape Cod. With the assistance of John Clapp, whom he engaged as his carpenter, Clark began the erection of vats and windmills and laid hollow logs to carry the water from the sea.

The first local resident to make salt by the solar evaporation of seawater was Captain George Bonum Nye, who after the Revolutionary War owned a large extent of the shore in the southern part of town. His salt works were located at the mouth of the harbor opposite Little Island. At first, Captain Nye only made enough salt to supply himself and a few neighbors. Later, he increased his production and began selling his salt all over New England. Every year in the fall, Nye filled an ox cart with salt and traveled to the Green Mountains to sell salt to the Vermonters. Before returning to Sippican, he usually swapped his pair of oxen for two pairs of steers.

Captain Nye's works were located at what is now called Nye's Wharf off Water Street. An April 22, 1908 entry in the account book of the village's general store (owned by Rowland Luce and Sons) showed that "Capt. Geo. B. Nye" settled his account "by 12 bushes salt" and again on December 9, "by 9 bushels salt." Stephen Delano also had one of the earlier saltworks in Sippican. It was located across from present-day 319 Delano Road on the Weweantic River.

At the height of salt manufacturing in Sippican there were more than 20 saltworks producing 20,000 bushels a year. The price of salt finally reached as much as $8 a bushel in 1783, and in 1806, more salt was manufactured in Sippican than any other community. This salt was shipped throughout the United States, the West Indies, and Europe, but the largest part was sent south in small coasting schooners that sailed from Marion each spring. Salt was also shipped to points on the Hudson River. The largest works, those of Ebenezer Holmes, were located at the landing in the village. The works of Bradford Bartlett, Stephen Hammond, Seth Hammond, John Clapp, Captain Handy, Deacon Clark, and David Hiller were also on the west side of the harbor. Out on Great Neck were the works of Seth Blankinship and Stephen Delano and Sons. At the head of the harbor, Captain Hammett and John Haskell owned works on Little Neck.

John Clapp, the carpenter who helped James Clark erect his works, afterwards purchased land and built vats to engage in the salt industry on his own account. His works eventually became one of the largest in town. The main part of Clapp's saltworks was located in a large field behind the future site of the Congregational Chapel. Saltworks were established from the Congregational Church, across Cottage Street, and through the grounds of Tabor Academy, Burr Brothers Boat

This 1900 photograph shows windmills, pumps, and vats at the Bush saltworks.

Yard, and farther north to the Railroad Station. East Marion also had saltworks, as did Charles Neck (present-day Converse Point). Salt vats also ran from the lower village to Route 6 and along Little Neck and Great Neck.

Though the solar salt industry of Massachusetts never reached the heights of the fisheries, whaling, and textile industries, it was certainly an important trade. The eventual decline of the salt industry, which continued until the 1840s, occurred for a number of reasons. The price of the pine from which the vats were made began to rise; the 1815 hurricane destroyed many saltworks; the salt duty was removed in the 1840s, opening up trade in foreign and domestic salt; salt mines were discovered in Pennsylvania; and the process of canning food was developed. Many homes in Marion were built with recycled lumber from the salt vats when they were dismantled.

These saltworks are located in Dartmouth, Massachusetts.

5. MARION AND ITS HURRICANES

Hurricanes have ravaged seaside towns throughout history, and Marion has been struck many times by these sometimes devastating storms. Beginning with the Pilgrims, these events were recorded for later generations to read about. Governor William Bradford of Plymouth Colony wrote the first report of a hurricane in these parts when he described the great tidal wave in Buzzards Bay in 1635.

The governor recorded that on August 14, there was such a mighty storm of wind and rain that no living English or native from this area ever saw such a "storme." It not only blew down houses, he said, but many vessels were lost at sea. Bradford described seas swelling to 20 feet and said that many "Indeans" climbed trees for their safety. He also described how a roof from a plantation in Manamet was blown off and floated to another place, leaving only posts still standing in the ground. He speculated that if the wind had not shifted when it did, "that it would have drounded some part of ye cuntrie."

Bradford also recorded that the 1635 hurricane blew down many hundred thousands of trees, turning some up by the roots and breaking the higher pine trees off in the middle, while winding tall, young oaks and large walnut trees like wreaths. He described these as very strange and fearful to behold and said that the results of this storm would remain for 100 years.

The next recorded hurricane is found in the diary of an anonymous Marion resident. He described the hurricane that occurred on Saturday, September 23, 1815, as beginning with a shower of rain from the east, then veering to the southeast with increased violence. Although high tide was scheduled for 11:30 a.m., the tide between 8:00 and 9:00 a.m. was as high as the highest spring tides and continued to increase in height and velocity. He said that at about 10:00 a.m. the tide water had covered all the mowing lands when the wind changed from southeast to south. He recorded that "such wind never was known on this coast." Another resident at the time, Frederick Freeman, noted that trees were uprooted in great numbers, buildings were "prostrated," saltworks destroyed, vessels scattered from their moorings and driven ashore, and vegetation destroyed in great measure. Freeman wrote that the tide rose 8 feet higher than normal in most areas, but in the bay, it was several feet higher still. He speculated that if the tide

These are the ruins of Watt's Boat Yard after the 1938 hurricane. Burr's Boat Yard stands here today.

had risen another 15 inches, "it would have passed completely over the isthmus of the Cape."

The saltworks that were located up and down the harbor in Marion were ruined in this storm, and many of the houses—which would hold their positions until the tide reached their roofs—were overturned and some floated across the harbor. The ruins of buildings were found in the woods at Wareham, including a store. Once located at Great Neck and containing West India goods, this store floated across to Wareham, where it came to rest with its goods in perfect preservation. Coasting vessels in the bay were drawn high on the shore—one floated among the forest trees in an upright position and was later re-launched.

The tide rose 8 feet above the common level, and many residents in the Upper Landing pounded nail heads high up on their houses to mark how far the water came up during what they called the "Great Gale." The spray resembled a driving snowstorm, and the grass was entirely killed. The leaves on the trees appeared scorched, and several cedar swamps perished. Wells and watering places for cattle were filled with seawater, and the saltiness of the wells near the sea remained that way until November. After the snows of the winter melted away, some wells became suddenly fresh again, while others did not recover for two years. In 1816, some of the overflowed fields were planted with oats and produced a larger crop than ever before. Mosses flourished and wild grasses grew where cultivated grass had once been.

But Marion suffered its worst hurricane in memory on September 21, 1938. Nothing in the experience of those living in New England had prepared them for the terror and disaster that was to be visited on them that day. It had been more than a century since a destructive storm had hit this area, and although there were warnings that a hurricane was approaching, there was no hint of the danger that was to be wrought by the 100-mile-per-hour gale. As the wind mounted during early afternoon, few realized that the hurricane of 1938 would be the costliest natural disaster in American history to that date.

The destructive impact of the storm was increased in New England by the fact that the tide was rising to its peak at the time the hurricane struck. Unfortunately, the tide was also at its highest point in the year due to the nearness of the autumnal equinox, when the sun and moon are both in line with the earth and so exert a double gravitational pull. These factors, in addition to the hurricane, which was driving the tide before it, forced water toward the coast. When the water hit the shallows of the continental shelf, the sea spilled onto the land with terrific force, almost as if it were an earthquake.

In late afternoon, the storm struck Marion with its full fury and many summerhouses were immediately swept from their foundations. Travelers were overwhelmed by rising tides as they rode in their cars. Boats were hurled far inland on highways, into forests, even inside buildings. The water rose 11.53 feet above normal high tide, and combined with the wind (which at times doubtless

The Russell Makepeace house, which stood just below Tabor Academy's Lillard Hall, is shown at the height of the 1938 hurricane. It still stands, but was later moved south on Front Street. Not only did the storm wash furniture out of the house, it also washed furniture from other homes on Ram Island into the house.

exceeded 100 miles per hour) swept all before it. The deluge swept away beaches, highways, and factories. It marooned workers, divided families, disrupted utilities, and caused such a loss of life as New England had never before experienced from a storm.

The hurricane continued to pound Marion until after 7:00 p.m. the same day and then moved on, carrying death and destruction with it. The path of the hurricane was approximately 400 miles, but only the 200-mile-long arm that extended eastward from near New York to the upper Cape received extensive damage. A high-pressure area to the west kept the main force of the storm confined to New England instead of letting it sweep over New York City, Philadelphia, and the New Jersey cities. Northern New England suffered extensive damage from the hurricane (though, fortunately, the storm merely touched Boston) and the damage likewise was extensive in Quebec. The storm continued north and most likely expended itself in the sub-Arctic wastes.

The losses in Marion exceeded $1.5 million, including the total destruction of the Beverly Yacht Club and other structures and the extensive property damage to many fine summer estates. Over one-quarter of the telephones were out of service, and the water on Bird Island was 16 feet deep. Additionally, Watts Boat Yard, which once stood where Burr Brothers Boat Yard is today, caught fire and burned during the hurricane. The official death toll for the region affected by this hurricane was fixed at 588, and experts estimated the total property loss at $400

The biggest tree in Marion—124 years old—had to be propped up to save the house on the left after the hurricane of 1944.

The Whistler *was washed onto the front lawn of Tabor Academy during the 1944 hurricane. Despite its unusual journey, it landed on an even keel.*

million (57,034 homes destroyed or damaged), making it the costliest storm in the United States on record at that time. The hurricane taught New England a new respect for modern storm warnings.

Just six years later, on September 14, 1944, another hurricane struck southeastern Massachusetts, bringing with it very strong winds. This time, however, adequate warning was given by the newspapers and radio, and beach residents left their homes before the storm struck. Winds increased rapidly between 9:00 and 10:00 p.m., and before midnight, they were blowing at 100 miles per hour. Accompanying rain became a blinding deluge, and once again, houses were blown or washed away, boats wrecked, trees ripped out, and plate-glass windows shattered. Thousands of houses were damaged by trees that crashed into them when uprooted by the gale, and famous elms, which had braved such storms for a century or more, were ripped out of the ground. Fortunately, this time high tide had passed nearly three hours before the gale struck, reducing the losses greatly.

Members of the state guard, Coast Guard, Red Cross, and Civilian Defense were organized to aid storm victims and to guard property. State guards were on duty for several days following the storm to protect damaged property and to patrol the darkened streets. Utilities suffered heavier damage to transmission lines than had been experienced in the storm of 1938 just six years earlier, as falling trees took hundreds of lines and cables down with them. It was a night of terror and destruction, yet this time only 31 deaths were reported.

This cruiser came to rest on Front Street in front of what is now the office of Burr Brothers Boat Yard.

On August 31, 1954, Hurricane Carol crashed ashore in Marion after having developed in the Bahamas several days earlier. Winds of 80 to 100 miles per hour roared through the eastern half of Connecticut, Rhode Island, and most of eastern Massachusetts, leaving 65 people dead when it was all over. Scores of trees and miles of power lines were blown down. The strongest wind ever recorded on Block Island, Rhode Island, occurred during Hurricane Carol, when winds gusted to 135 miles per hour.

Hurricane Carol arrived shortly after high tide in Marion, causing widespread tidal flooding. Storm surge levels ranged from 10 to 15 feet. As in 1938, storm tides increased just before landfall with over 14-foot surges in the harbor, and rainfall amounts were recorded at 6 inches in some areas. Hurricane Carol destroyed nearly 4,000 homes, along with 3,500 automobiles and more than 3,000 boats. Electric and telephone service was interrupted in Marion and other areas in eastern Massachusetts. Carol was the most destructive hurricane to strike southern New England since 1938.

On Friday, September 27, 1985, Hurricane Gloria's track put it very close to Buzzards Bay. With knowledge of the storm that was to come, residents rushed to get boats out of the water on Wednesday. Owners and boatyard workers spent long hours hauling, securing, and adding chafing to the mooring pennants of boats that were remaining in the water. When the hurricane struck on Friday,

Gloria's winds gusted up to 90 miles per hour in Marion Harbor. The storm worsened when the wind swung to the south and the tide rose too high. Boats snapped their shortened pennants and, one by one, 62 boats sailed free and careened drunkenly up the harbor to wind up in the marsh or on the rocks. Even those vessels that didn't break loose were threatened by the pilot-less drifters coming down on them.

By Saturday, the salvage task began, but many boats were out of reach, strewn about in the marshes at an impossible distance from the harbor. Some close enough to water were salvaged by a barge-mounted crane. One boat, *Tempest,* found resting against trees at the far edge of the marsh, was sold "as is, where is." A number of other boats could not be moved without doing unacceptable damage to the marsh. Burr Brothers Boat Yard came up with a plan that utilized a sky crane helicopter from Erikson Air-Crane Company, based in Oregon, to remove some 25 boats.

In an effort fully supported by Barden's Boat Yard, Aucoot Boat Yard, the Wareham Boat Yard, the Marion harbormaster, and the Police and Fire Departments, an 88-foot Sikorsky S64E helicopter was flown in from a Detroit job. Its two 4,500-horsepower engines whirled 72-foot blades to lift up to 20,000 pounds. The preparation was so exact that 25 boats were moved in less than three hours of flying time. Airlifted boats in Marion included the following: *Acapella,*

Henry P. Kendall's boat Louise *washed ashore during Hurricane Carol and onto his neighbor Miss Austin's property on Water Street. Austin is claimed to have had Kendall arrested for trespassing.*

The Burr Brothers Boat Yard developed a pioneering salvage method after Hurricane Gloria in 1985. This Sikorski Skycrane helicopter from the Erikson Air-Crane Company moved 25 boats in less than three hours.

Affinity, Allegro, Birkett, Cirrus, Fancy Free, Gaudior, Hoo Nu Too, Lynn IV, Magic Dragon, Margaret D, Messing About, North Star, Prince Henry, Puppy Love, Seiour, Second Lady, Shimbumi, Sisu, Tigger, Tiger Too, Trade Winds, Xenobia, and *Yukon Jack.* The cost for this salvage process was approximately $3,000 per boat, and the method represented a significant improvement in both cost and amount of damage sustained by boats. Marion was a pioneer in this airlifting salvage system.

Hurricane Bob, which struck on August 19, 1991, was not as severe as previous storms, but those who suffered loss remember it as an important event in Marion history. Because of better warnings from the National Hurricane Center and the fact that the storm was weakening when it hit, only 17 lives were lost to Hurricane Bob.

However, the insurance industry at the time ranked Hurricane Bob as the second most expensive hurricane ever reported, with damage to insured property set at $780 million. It was also the earliest in the season to strike New England, thus causing severe marine losses because of its arrival at the height of the boating season. Heavy rains occurred throughout New England with 14.25 inches reported in Wakefield, Massachusetts.

The usually safe harbor of Marion was heavily damaged by Hurricane Bob, and Harbormaster George Jennings noted that nearly all of the town's 850 moorings had dislodged or needed replotting. A 600-foot section of Point Road and 1,300 feet of the Planting Island causeway were damaged and required $200,000 in repairs. Eleven floats near Old Landing and Island Wharf were swept away, and a grand total of $668,000 was spent to clean up after the hurricane.

The tides reached 8 to 10 feet above normal and approximately one-half of the 850 boats in Marion Harbor were damaged. Many boats were driven ashore and at least two were driven far ashore in Aucoot Cove. Forty-five boats still remained on shore on August 30, some of them so large that they could not be airlifted. At least 100 boats broke loose as the tidal surge occurred. Boats and docks were strewn across the shoreline of the Beverly Yacht Club. Tabor Academy was also damaged when a boat smashed against Daggett House, where seawater had risen at least halfway up the first-floor walls, and Kittansett Club on Point Road was flooded with 4 feet of water. The windows of the club's pro shop were blown out and a 3-foot blanket of sea grass was left behind. One hundred twenty people sought shelter at the Sippican Elementary School.

Despite the fact that Marion has been struck many times by hurricanes, it has always cleaned up, rebuilt, and got on with its affairs. Residents have concluded that the benefits of living in this small seaside community far outweigh the occurrences of the hurricanes that have ravaged it from time to time. They have decided most definitely to stay put.

Hurricane Bob waters the lawn, porch, and junior clubhouse at the Beverly Yacht Club on August 19, 1991.

79

6. HMS NIMROD

During the War of 1812, the British warship HMS *Nimrod*, which had orders to enforce the blockade of American shipping along the coasts of Cape Cod, Martha's Vineyard, Nantucket, Rhode Island, and Connecticut, destroyed and captured many American vessels. On January 29, 1814, the *Nimrod* (the name is taken from the Bible and means "skillful hunter") bombarded Falmouth. Before the assault, however, a Tarpaulin Cove innkeeper overheard a group of British officers discussing the attack and their plan to capture two brass cannons from a Nantucket sloop that had fired upon them. The *Nimrod* showed up off Falmouth, where the local militia was well dug in, and was defied by the American Captain Weston Jenkins, who invited the British to "come and get it." The *Nimrod* responded with a bombardment that damaged 30 homes, but it departed the next morning without its intended prize: the cannons of the Nantucket sloop.

On June 13, 1814—as Marion lore recounts—the British ship anchored in Buzzards Bay about 4 miles from Bird Island and sent a raiding party with 6 barges and 200 men to Wareham, where they were to set vessels in the harbor on fire and burn a cotton mill. Twelve vessels were set on fire, including five that were completely destroyed. The story relates that the *Nimrod* then ran aground off Bird Island, and in order to lighten her load dumped her cannons and guns overboard. She then floated free and sailed away. Despite many years of searching for these fabled cannons off Bird Island, none were ever found.

The late Henry W. Kendall, a Nobel Prize–winning Massachusetts Institute of Technology physicist and longtime Marion summer resident, as well as an expert scuba diver, was very interested in the story of the HMS *Nimrod* and in the cannons that were purportedly dumped in Marion's harbor. Kendall's student at MIT and fellow diving enthusiast David W. Schloerb decided to do further research into where the cannons might be and spent about a month in the New Bedford Free Public Library reviewing newspapers from 1814. He also obtained copies of the logs of the HMS *Nimrod* from the Public Record Office in England.

After reading the logs of the *Nimrod*, Schloerb determined that the ship went aground off Great Ledge in Buzzards Bay on June 14, 1814, and that the cannons were thrown overboard there and not off Bird Island in Marion. It seems the *Nimrod* had attempted to attack New Bedford, came through Quick's Hole, and got stuck.

This illustration of the HMS Nimrod *was drawn by William C. Grant and is held in the Sippican Historical Society's museum.*

In August 1981, Kendall and Schloerb went diving to explore Great Ledge in Buzzards Bay. They anchored in the middle of Great Ledge and determined that there was about a square mile where the cannons would be. They swam along the depth that a ship would have gone aground and Schloerb put his hand on something that felt like a cannon. They brought it up and discovered that it indeed was one of the cannons from the *Nimrod*. Later, the pair returned to the area with a metal detector and found four more cannons, as well as a rare caronade, a small, muzzle-loading cannon mounted on a swivel that had a tiller for arming. It weighed 100 pounds, was 1.5 feet long, and could be carried by and fired from a small boat. The other cannons, weighing 600 to 700 pounds each, were recovered under a permit through the Massachusetts Board of Underwater Archaeological Resources. They were taken to Sippican Harbor in Marion and submerged in shallow saltwater. If taken out of the water and exposed to the air, the cannons would have quickly rusted away. Instead, they were kept in fiberglass-lined boxes filled with water and an alkaline additive to counteract the acidic effects of the saltwater. Over time, the alkaline baths would stabilize the iron and the cannons could be removed.

Two cannons were taken to the Kendall Whaling Museum in Sharon, Massachusetts, which had been established by Henry Kendall's parents, Henry P. and Evelyn L. Kendall, in 1956. One cannon went to the Wareham Public Library. Another, weighing approximately 800 pounds, was given to the Falmouth Historical Society to display at its historic house museums near the town's village green. Another was given to the Stonington Lighthouse Museum in Stonington, Connecticut, which the HMS *Nimrod* also raided.

Despite not finding the cannons within its waters, Marion is proud that one of its longtime residents finally solved the mystery of the jettisoned cannons. At long last, they have been retrieved from the deep and are on public display for history buffs to view.

David W. Schloerb (left) and the late Henry W. Kendall pose with the first of five cannons from the HMS Nimrod that they recovered off Great Ledge in Buzzards Bay. This photograph was taken at Burr Brothers Boat Yard in Marion in August 1981. (Courtesy David W. Schloerb.)

The HMS Nimrod jettisons artillery in this drawing by artist William Gilkerson.

7. BIRD ISLAND LIGHTHOUSE

On May 3, 1819, George Blankinship of Rochester sold Bird Island, a 1.5-acre island in Buzzards Bay about 3 miles from Marion Village, to the U.S. government for $200. A lighthouse was built there, which was established on March 1819 by an Act of Congress. It was operational and lit for the first time on September 10, 1819. Congress allocated $4,040 for the construction of the stone house and light.

Bird Island Light was the 59th lighthouse built in the United States, and it was established because of the heavy commercial flow in and out of Buzzards Bay and Sippican Harbor due to the whaling and salt industries in the area. The light was 25 feet high and 18 feet in diameter. It had 3-foot-thick stone walls and a 12-foot iron lantern at the top.

The keeper's house was 20 feet by 34 feet and included two fireplaces, a porch, a well and cistern, a covered walk to the light, and an "upstairs gable facing the light to facilitate the keeper's vigilance." The specifications for Bird Island Lighthouse were set forth in the Articles of Agreement on May 4, 1819, as follows:

> The Light House to be built of Stone, the form round; the foundations to be sunk as deep as may be found necessary to render the fabric secure laid in good lime mortar; the height of the Tower to be twenty-five feet from the surface of the ground; the diameter of the base eighteen feet, and that of the top ten feet, the thickness of the walls at the base three feet, uniformly graduated to twenty inches at the top, the outside to be faced with split, undressed stone, painted and white washed twice over; the top of the Tower to be arched, on which is to be laid a soap stone deck, twelve feet in diameter, four inches thick, on one side of which is to be a scuttle to enter the lantern; the scuttle door to be framed with iron and covered with copper, the joints of the stone deck to be fitted with lead; there must be three windows in the tower each of twelve lights of ten by eight glass with strong frames and a door five feet by three made from double inch boards, cross nailed with substantial hinges, lock with latch the ground floor to be paved with brick or stone;

a sufficient number of circular stairs to lead from the ground floor within six feet of the top; the stairs guarded by a strong hand railing; one iron ladder from the top of the stairs to the entrance of the scuttle, with steps two inches wide. An iron lantern of an octagon form, the posts to be one and three quarter inches square and to run down into the stonework five feet; the height and diameter to be sufficient to admit an iron sash in each octagon to contain twenty-one lights, twelve by ten; the lower tier to be filled with copper; the rabbets of the sashes to be three-quarters of an inch deep and to be glazed with the best double glass from the Boston Manufactory; in one of the octagons an iron framed door covered with copper four feet by two to shut tight into rabbets with two strong turn buttons; the top to be a dome formed by sixteen iron rafters concentrating into an iron hoop four inches wide and nine inches in diameter covered with thirty ounce copper which must come down and meet on the piece that forms the top of the sash which is to be three inches wide: on the top a traversing ventilator two and a half feet long and fifteen inches in diameter on which must be secured a copper vane

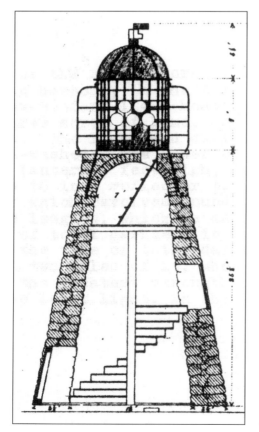

This is a cross-section from the plans for the Bird Island Lighthouse, built in 1819.

three feet long and twenty inches wide; the lantern to be guarded by an iron railing, the posts to be one and one quarter inches square, the upper one to be four feet above the deck the lighthouse to have one complete electrical conductor made of copper three quarters of an inch in diameter with a point, the lantern door and windows of the tower to be painted twice over with white lead, except the dome which is to be painted black.

A stone dwelling, thirty four feet by twenty, one story of eight feet high divided into two rooms with an entry between; the stairs to be in the entry to go into the chambers which are to be lathed and plastered, a chimney near the middle of the house with a fireplace in each room, iron or stone mantelpieces, cellar under the whole of the house with sufficient walls of stone laid in lime mortar, twenty inches thick, six feet deep, the walls of the house to be twenty inches thick laid up in lime mortar with split undressed stone, well pointed, and white washed twice over, the roof to be rectangular, the boards of which to be jointed and halved and well secured and covered with good merchantable shingles. Three windows in each room of sixteen lights of eight by ten glass each and one of the same dimensions in each chamber, the doors to be four paneled with good hinges and thumb latches to each and a good lock on the outside door; closets in each room back of the chimney; all the floors to be double and well nailed – the inside walls and ceilings to be lathed and plastered, and all the inside work to be finished in a plain decent style, with good seasoned lumber.

Also a porch attached to the dwelling house fourteen feet by twelve in the clear; the walls of stone eight feet high the room to be lathed and plastered, with double floors two windows and one door, a chimney with a fireplace and an oven with an iron door, crane trammels and hooks in the fireplace in the porch; one side of the chimney a sink with a spout leading through the stone wall. All the wood work inside and out to be painted with two good coats of paint; gutters to lead round the house with spouts to carry off the water; an out-house five feet by four shingled and painted; a well sufficiently deep to procure good water; stoned and bricked up with a good curb and windlass; with an iron chain and a strong iron hoped bucket; the whole to be finished in a workman like manner by the first of September next.

Bird Island Lighthouse was the sole lighthouse in Buzzards Bay until 1837, when a land-based lighthouse was constructed in Mattapoisett.

Edmund M. Blunt's 1827 book *The American Coast Pilot* described Bird Island and its light for seacoast vessels in the following way:

Bird Island is on the north shore of Buzzard's Bay, near the east side of Sippican harbour, in the town of Rochester, about 12 miles E.N.E. from

The Bird Island Lighthouse appears here in 1910 with all its outbuildings.

New-Bedford light-house. It is small, not containing more than three acres of land, and is about five feet above the level of the sea. The light and dwelling-houses are built of stone, and are white-washed. The tower of the former is 25 feet high, on which is a lantern 7 feet high, that is lighted with 10 patent lamps, with a 16 inch reflector to each, fitted on two sides of an oblong square, which revolves round once in 3 minutes, at the distance of five leagues, which is as far as it can be seen for the land. The time of total darkness is twice to that of light. As you approach it, the time of total darkness increases, until you get within two miles of it, when there will not be a total darkness, but the greatest strength of light will be as 40 to 1 over that of the least light, in the course of the revolution of the apparatus.

The first lighthouse keeper on Bird Island was William Moore, who, as the generally accepted story goes, was given the position as punishment for some crime. He was reportedly a convicted criminal and pirate who was sent to the island with his poor wife and son. They lived as prisoners and were not allowed a boat to come to shore. Captain Blankinship of Marion took food, mail, and necessary supplies to the Moores from time to time. Report has it that Mrs. Moore tried to escape from the island three times, but each time her husband frustrated her attempt. A grave on the island is said to be her final resting place.

The keepers of Bird Island Light were U.S. government employees. Some came alone, but others brought their families to the island with them. In the early years, the children of keepers would remain on the island, but in later years they boarded in Marion Village so they could attend school. The keepers lived very remote lives, rowing into Marion every couple of weeks for supplies and mail. Sometimes a Marion resident would take supplies out to Bird Island too. The keepers and their families kept a cow and poultry, cultivated vegetable gardens, and also fished.

Since communication was limited to actual contact with others, keeper Zimri Robinson devised a system of communication with townsfolk by installing a flagpole on the island. He flew a flag from it every day. The villagers understood that if the flag were hoisted upside down, it meant there was sickness or some other emergency on the island. People ashore kept watch and help was never long in coming when it was needed.

Once during Robinson's occupancy, the whole island was under water for about an hour. It was the highest tide any keeper had experienced on Bird Island. Robinson kept his boats from washing away by mooring them to his back porch. On another occasion, an extremely low tide permitted him to wade from Bird Island to Ruggles Point (near present-day Kittansett Club) without once getting his head under water.

Robinson also received an official commendation for an act of heroism while he was keeper of Bird Island. On September 30, 1907, he rescued Ernest Maxim

A bird's-eye view shows the Bird Island Lighthouse after the 1938 hurricane.

of Middleboro and two companions who were drifting helplessly in Buzzards Bay. Robinson went to their rescue "in the teeth of a northeast gale," after sighting them a mile out from the island. They had run out of fuel for their power boat, tried to anchor, and lost their anchor in the heavy seas. Robinson took with him a large anchor with plenty of line, a basket of food, a can of milk, and a can of water. The men had drifted all night across the bay before being rescued.

The following information on the identities and salaries of the lighthouse keepers at Bird Island appeared in government records in the years listed:

1819	William Moore	$300 per year
1834	John Clark	$350 per year
1835	John Clark	$400 per year
1849	James Delano	$400 per year
1861	Marshall V. Simmons	$400 per year
1872	Charles A. Clark Sr.	$560 per year
1889	Charles A. Clark Jr.	$560 per year
1891	Peter Murray	$560 per year
1895	Zimri T. Robinson	$560 per year
1912	E.C. Hardley Jr.	$600 per year
1917	H.H. Davis	$600 per year
1919	M.A. Babcock	$600 per year
1926	George T. Gustavus	$600 per year
1933	*station closed*	

Other interesting lighthouse-related documents have survived, including a letter dated December 13, 1883, that was sent to keeper Charles A. Clark Sr. by G.H. Wadleigh, inspector of the Second Light House District. This letter discussed the acquisition of uniforms for keepers. Another document warned of the danger of cholera washing up on shore in the form of infected garbage and asked keepers to burn anything they found on the beaches.

In 1911, Marion resident Matilda Allen Parshley wrote a small booklet entitled *Stories of Bird Island*, in which she collected the legends and lore of the lonely parcel of land. One story, "The Bird Island Pirate," speculates on the origin and not-so-fine character of the light's first keeper, William Moore:

> The first light keeper took charge of the Island about the time of the War of 1812. The townspeople whispered that he was a pirate and an outlaw, and certainly his wife lived a sad and lonely life enough. His wife was a Boston beauty of prominent family, who eloped with her pirate cavalier one dark and stormy night, and after various changes of fortune, they came in charge of this lonely little island, set like a beautiful emerald in the circle of the land-locked harbor.
>
> By this time Mrs. Moore's beauty and her hopes had faded, and she would have had a cruel enough time, if the kindly townspeople had

not practiced all kinds of devices to smuggle her solaces, snuff and tobacco to her. For as she was wasting with consumption, these were [her] only relief.

Once, with the aid of these same kind friends, she made her escape to Ruggles' Point, where old Captain Blankinship was prepared to defend her with his life, but her husband followed her and pleaded eloquently that she abandon her plan of returning to her own people. Her pirate husband took her back to that emerald prison which she never was to leave again, until the dark angel came to her rescue. Not long afterward the townspeople heard of her death, and it was whispered that he killed her. There was a lonely burial on the Island.

When the quaint old stone house with its tiny windows was pulled down to make room for a frame building, a secret cupboard was discovered containing someone with glittering veins, a bag of snuff, and a paper calling down the curses of heaven on those people who had aided and abetted Moore's wife. Soon after his wife's death Moore and his son disappeared and were never heard of after.

Bird Island Lighthouse was closed by an Act of Congress in 1933 after having been in continuous operation for 115 years. The light suffered heavy damage in

Zimri T. Robinson is at far right in this photograph taken at the base of the lighthouse around the start of his tenure as keeper, 1895–1912.

the 1938 hurricane, and the keeper's house and outbuildings were completely destroyed, leaving only the stone lighthouse tower and the foundation of the house. In 1940, Bird Island was sold for $645 to George Harmon of Bar Harbor, and then again that same year to Augustus Fiske. In 1966, the Town of Marion acquired Bird Island from Augustus Fiske's heirs for $2,500. With the assistance of the Sippican Historical Society, funds were raised to restore Bird Island Lighthouse, and the beacon was re-lit in 1976 as part of the town's bicentennial celebration. Today, Bird Island Light is not only one of Marion's most visible landmarks, but also a welcoming sign to sailors from around the world. It also serves as a sanctuary for roseate terns.

Bird Island light showing the high-water mark of the 1938 hurricane. All of the lighthouse's outbuildings were destroyed in the storm.

8. MARY CELESTE

One of the most widely known of all marine mysteries began in Marion: the tale of the "ghost ship" *Mary Celeste*. Her captain, Benjamin Spooner Briggs, lived in Marion with his wife, Sarah Elizabeth Briggs, and their two children, Arthur Stanley, age 7, and Sophia Matilda, age 2.

On October 19, 1872, Captain Briggs left his home at Rose Cottage in Sippican Village for New York to supervise the loading of the half-brig *Mary Celeste*, of which he owned a one-third interest. The ship was to carry a cargo of 1,700 barrels of alcohol valued at $38,000 to Genoa, Italy. After delivering the alcohol to Genoa the vessel was chartered to carry a return cargo of fruit from Messina to New York.

A week after Briggs arrived in New York, his wife and daughter joined him there in order to travel with him on the trip. Prior to this, Sarah had had her sewing machine and melodeon shipped to New York to accompany them on the long voyage.

Arthur Stanley was left with his grandmother in Marion so that he could continue his schooling. Captain Briggs and his wife looked forward to the trip, which promised to be financially profitable for them. Raised in a sea-faring family, Briggs was well prepared to undertake the responsibilities of command of the *Mary Celeste*.

On November 3, 1872, two days before the vessel was to set sail for Genoa, Captain Briggs wrote to his mother in Marion:

> My dear Mother:
>
> It is a long time since I have written you a letter and I should like to give a real interesting one but I hardly know what to say except that I am well and the rest of us ditto, it is such a long time since I composed other than business epistles. It seems to me to have been a great while since I left home, but it is only little over two weeks but in that time my mind has been filled with business cares and I am again launched away into the busy whirl of business life from which I have so long been laid aside. For a few days it was tedious, perplexing, and very tiresome but now I have

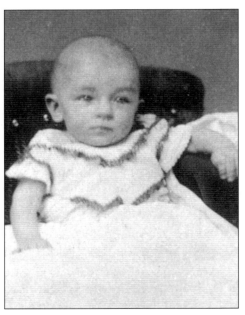

The Briggs family members are, clockwise from top left, Captain Benjamin Spooner Briggs, master of the Mary Celeste; *Sophia Matilda Briggs, his daughter; Sarah Briggs, his wife; and Arthur Stanley Briggs, the son of Captain and Mrs. Briggs, who did not join the rest of the family on the mysterious voyage in 1872.*

got fairly settled down to it and it sets lightly and seems to run more smoothly and my appetite keeps good and I hope I shan't lose any flesh. It seems real homelike since Sarah and Sophia got here, and we enjoy our little quarters. On Thurs. we had a call from Willis and his wife. Took Sophia and went with them on a ride up to Central Park. Sophia behaved splendid and seemed to enjoy the ride as much as any of us. It was the only time that they have been away from the vessel. On account of the horse disease the horse cars have not been running on this side of the city, so we have not been able to go and make any calls as we were so far away from any one to go on foot and to hire a private carriage would have cost us at least $10.00 a trip which we didn't feel able to pay and we couldn't walk and carry Sophia a mile or two which we should have had to do to get to a ferry for Ivamacs or E-port. It has been very confining for S. but I hope when we return, we can make up for it. We seem to have a very good mate and steward and I hope shall have a pleasant voyage. We both have missed Arthur and I believe I should have sent for him if I could have thought of a good place to stow him away. Sophia calls for him occasionally and wants to see him in the Album which by the way is a favorite book of hers. She knows your picture in both Albums and points and says Gamma Bis. She seems real smart, has got over her bad cold she had when she came and has a first rate appetite for hash and bread and butter. I think the voyage will do her lots of good. We enjoy our melodeon and have some good sings. I was in hopes Oli might get in before I left but am afraid not now. We finished loading last night and shall leave on Tuesday morning if we don't get off tomorrow night, the Lord willing. Our vessel is in beautiful trim and I hope we shall have a fine passage but as I have never been in her before can't say how she'll sail. Shall want you to write us in about 20 days to Genoa, care of Am. Counsel and about 20 days after to Messina care of Am. Consul who will forward to us if we don't go there. I wrote James to pay you for A's board and rent. If he forgets call on him also for any money that may be necessary for clothes. Please get Eben to see his skates are all right and the holes in his new thick boot heels. I hope he'll keep well as I think if he does he'll be some help as well as company for you. Love to Hannah. Sophie calls Aunt Hannah often. I wish we had a picture so she could remember the countenance as well as name.

Hoping to be with you again early in the spring with much love I am

Yours affectionately
Benj

(postscript written top of page)
Shall leave Tuesday morning.

Rose Cottage in Marion was the boyhood home of Captain Benjamin Spooner Briggs.

The *Mary Celeste* cleared New York on November 4, 1872. On board were Captain Benjamin S. Briggs, Mate Albert G. Richardson, Second Mate Andrew Gilling, Cook E.W. Head, Seamen Vokert Lorenzeau, Arien Harhens, Bos Larensen, and Gottlieb Goodschoad, along with the captain's wife and two-year-old daughter. On November 5, the ship left the East River Pier in New York and anchored off Staten Island because of unfavorable weather. On November 7, "with wind light but favorable," she weighed anchor and proceeded on her voyage.

While waiting for more favorable weather in which to begin their journey, Mrs. Briggs also wrote to her mother-in-law in Marion:

Brig *Mary Celeste*
Off Staten Island, Nov. 7th

Dear Mother Briggs,

Probably you will be a little surprised to receive a letter with this date, but instead of proceeding to sea when we came out Tuesday morning, we anchored about a mile or so from the city, as it was strong head wind, and B. said it looked so thick and nasty ahead we shouldn't gain much if we were beating and banging about. Accordingly we took a fresh departure this morning with wind light but favorable, so we hope to get outside without being obliged to anchor. Have kept sharp lookout for Oliver, but so far have seen nothing of him. It was rather trying to lay in sight of the city so long and think that most likely we had letters waiting for us there, and be unable to get them. However, we hope no great change has occurred since we did hear and shall look for a goodly supply when we reach G. [Genoa].

Sophy thinks the figure 3 and the letter G on her blocks is the same thing so I saw her whispering to herself yesterday with the 3 block in her hand—gam-gam-gamma.

Benj. thinks we have got a pretty peaceable set this time all around, if they continue as they have begun. Can't tell yet how smart they are.

B. reports a good breeze now, says we are going along nicely.

I should like to be present at Mr. Kingsbury's ordination next week. Hope the people will be united in him, and wish we might hear of Mrs. K's improved health on arrival.

Tell Arthur I make great dependence on the letter I shall get from him and will try to remember anything that happens on the voyage which he would be pleased to hear.

We had some baked apples (sour) the other night abut the size of a newborn infant's head. They tasted extremely well.

Please give our love to mother and the girls, Aunt Hannah, Arthur, and other friends, reserving a share for yourself.

As I have nothing more to say, I will follow A. Ward's advice and say it at once.

Farewell,
Yours affectionately,
Sarah

The half-brig Amazon, *later renamed* Mary Celeste, *appears in an unsigned 1861 painting.*

On November 15, 1872, the British brigantine *Dei Gratia* sailed from New York, only eight days after the *Mary Celeste*. On December 5, Captain Morehouse of the *Dei Gratia* saw the *Mary Celeste* headed westerly with a northerly wind in the waters between the Azores and the coast of Portugal. As it was evident to him that something was wrong on board the *Mary Celeste*, he sent his mate Oliver Deveau to investigate.

Deveau found no one on board. The yawl boat was gone, the binnacle on its side, the compass broken, the fore sail and upper top-sail evidently blown away, and the forehatch off and laying upside down on the deck. The beds were made and a pillow bore the impress of a child's head as if it had just been sleeping there. A small garment was on the sewing machine. A drawer containing canned goods was open and the contents in disorder. The ship's papers, the chronometer, and sextant were gone. The two compasses, the Captain's watch, and a sum of money in his desk remained, and money was also found in the chests of three of the sailors.

Although the *Mary Celeste* was abandoned, it was noted that it was generally seaworthy, but wandering ghostlike without master or crew. The vessel was well provisioned with food and water and the hull, spars, and standing rigging were in good order. With the exception of two sails blown away, the vessel appeared fit to go around the world, according to the crew of the *Dei Gratia*.

In a wood engraving by Rudolph Ruzicka, this is how the abandoned Mary Celeste *appeared when first sighted by the* Dei Gratia *on December 4, 1872.*

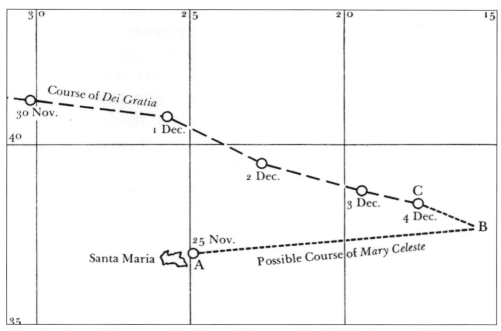

Above is a chart of the courses of the Mary Celeste *and the* Dei Gratia *east of the Azores.*

The last entry in the ship's log had been made several days before in the Azores near Saint Mary's Island on November 25, 1872 at 8:00 a.m.: "At 8, Eastern point bore SSW. 6 miles distant." The vessel's log also contained an observation taken at noon on the prior day: "Sunday, 24 November Latitude 36° 56' North, Longitude 27° 20' West." When found ten days later, the vessel was 600 miles east of the position given on November 24. She must have sailed east most of this time, lost two sails, and turned around shortly before being found. The vessel had evidently been hurriedly abandoned, perhaps in a moment of panic.

Since 1872, there has been endless speculation as to what happened to the Briggs family and the crew of seven aboard the *Mary Celeste*. No one knows why the vessel was so hastily abandoned. Mutiny was ruled out because there was no sign of violence aboard the ship. Other theories include storms, seaquakes, piracy, icebergs, and foul play.

Some think that the warm weather made the 1,700 barrels of alcohol expand, that gasses began to rumble in the hold, and that the captain was afraid of a disastrous explosion. Thus, he launched the boat and tied it to the peak halyard as a towrope. The wind may have then come up and the *Mary Celeste* carried away, leaving eight men, a woman, and a child in a small boat on the open ocean. Others think that a sudden squall came up and sank the small craft.

After an inquiry at Gibraltar, the *Dei Gratia* was given a partial salvage award for finding the derelict ship. To this day, the story of the brig *Mary Celeste* remains one of the greatest unsolved mysteries in maritime history.

9. The Beverly Yacht Club

One of the oldest yacht clubs in the country, the Beverly Yacht Club was organized in 1872 by Walter Burgess, a younger brother of the famous yacht designer Edward Burgess. Walter and Edward Burgess were ardent sailors and were unhappy that the Eastern Yacht Club in Marblehead had refused to recognize yachts under 26 feet long at the water line in its races that summer. At the suggestion of Benjamin F. Burgess, the father of Walter and Edward, the men invited their young friends on the north shore of Boston to a dinner at their home at 62 Beacon Street in Boston on February 24, 1872, where the new club for racing smaller yachts was formally launched.

Beverly Yacht Club began as a racing organization serving Massachusetts Bay and Buzzards Bay sailors and gradually focused more specifically on Buzzards Bay until it settled in Marion for good. Through the years, the club's tradition of small boat racing has been maintained but it took a while to settle on a permanent home.

Besides Edward, Sidney, Arthur, and Walter Burgess, also present at the initial meeting were Count Nicola Altrochi, John F. Andrew, William Appleton, Perry Belmont, T. Dennie Boardman, Arthur W. Cabot, Abbot W. Cobb, Edward W. Codman, Franklin Dexter, Edward Everett, George Fiske, George A. Gibson, William A. Jeffries, Walter Lloyd Jeffries, Henry W. Lamb, William Lawrence, Lewis Cass Ledyard, William Caleb Loring, Harrison Gray Otis, Dudley M. Pickman, Edward B. Russell, David Sears Jr., Alanson Tucker, Frank M. Weld, George West, Edward F. Whitney, William F. Whitney, and Charles H. Williams. The name "Beverly" was chosen as the name of the new organization (the town of Beverly, Massachusetts is where the Burgesses' summer home was located), with Edward Burgess as its first commodore for a two-year term. In its early years, the group was more in the nature of a yacht racing organization rather than a regular yacht club. Dues were $5 a year.

The Beverly Yacht Club began running races along the north shore of Boston for smaller yachts. The first regatta was held at Beverly on June 22, 1872, and five other regattas were held during that season: one at South Boston, another at Swampscott, and three more at Beverly. For the first 23 years, the club had no fixed location. It held regattas around the north shore in Beverly, Swampscott,

Nahant, and Marblehead. It also ran races in South Boston and Cohasett and in various Buzzards Bay locations off Monument Beach, West Falmouth, Quissett, and Marion.

In 1893, Mrs. M.C. Van Rensselaer of New York, a summer resident, offered a cup in memory of her son George Graham Van Rensselaer, who had drowned the year before. Races for the Van Rensselaer Memorial Cup have been held annually since 1896 by the Beverly Yacht Club.

As the Beverly Yacht Club's Buzzards Bay membership increased, the organization finally leased a house in 1895 at Wing's Neck across Buzzards Bay from Marion in Bourne and ran races from there. The club purchased the Wing's Neck house four years later.

The problems of the proximity of the Cape Cod Canal, the lower channel of which crossed the starting line off the Wing's Neck facility, caused the club to consider a better location. The members purchased land at the end of Butler's Point (sometimes called Ruggles' Point) in Marion, and a clubhouse was erected there in 1913.

Soon after, the Sippican Yacht Club, based in Marion, merged with the Beverly Yacht Club. The Sippican Yacht Club was founded in 1877 and incorporated in 1902. Its clubhouse, built in 1910, consisted of a two-story pavilion at the end of a substantial stone pier located south of Silvershell Beach. For a number of years, Beverly Yacht Club regattas were held in Marion in cooperation with the Sippican Yacht Club. When the two clubs merged into the Beverly Yacht Club in 1913, the Sippican pavilion stood derelict until it finally burned down sometime in the early

The Wing's Neck club house of the Beverly Yacht Club is pictured here in 1895.

Nine brand-new Herreshoff Buzzard's bay 30-footers (47 feet overall) cross the starting line off Wing's Neck in 1902.

1930s. Rumor has it that Parker "Rip" Converse and his brother Roger "Govey" Converse called the fire station to report a fire at the pavilion. When asked when the fire started, they replied, "We haven't started it yet." In any event, it would probably never have survived the 1938 hurricane.

From the new clubhouse of the Beverly Yacht Club at Butler's Point, spectators could view the races from start to finish—not only races for small yachts, but also for the M-class (90 feet) in 1928 and for the two former America's Cup contenders, *Vanitie* (118 feet) and *Resolute* (100 feet), in the following year. From the clubhouse, a long wooden pier extended out into the harbor and was used as one end of the starting line. It provided a starting line for winds in any direction. It was also a safe place to moor because it was sheltered in the lee of Bird Island and Butler's Point. Rooms at the clubhouse could be rented for $1 a day, and for an additional $1, the club supplied tea, coffee, milk, butter, bread, oatmeal, potatoes, sugar, and salt.

Disaster struck when the clubhouse and pier were completely destroyed on September 21, 1938, during the devastating hurricane. The water rose 11.5 feet above mean high water. Subsequently, Beverly Yacht Club members were given the privilege of using the Kittansett Club winter house. In fact, an addition was constructed there for use by the members of the Beverly Yacht Club.

During World War II, the U.S. Army occupied Butler's Point for "coast defense" and used the Kittansett winter clubhouse for quartering Army personnel. Another hurricane in 1944 did almost as much damage to the Kittansett winter clubhouse as the Army did. During the period from 1942 to 1946, the racing activities of the yacht club were restricted. At first, races were started and finished at Nye's Wharf in Sippican Harbor. Then a starting line was set around Planting Island. The regular Sunday and Wednesday races were held in the harbor as usual.

In 1950, the club arranged to lease a new clubhouse that was to be erected at Barden's Boat Yard. Unfortunately, Hurricane Carol, which arrived on August 31, 1954, completely demolished this building, and all of the club's records were lost. Subsequently, the owners of the house at the end of Main and Water Streets where Admiral Harwood once summered decided to sell, and certain members of the Beverly Yacht Club raised the necessary funds to purchase the home. This became the new clubhouse. Its pier, floats, and convenient location for visiting sailors made this location ideal, and the club has remained on the site ever since.

Two distinguished yacht designers have played an important role in the club's history: Edward Burgess, the club's first commodore; and Nathanael Herreshoff, the designer of some of Beverly Yacht Club's most important classes. Burgess became the leading American yacht designer in the 1880s and designed three successive America's Cup winners in 1885, 1886, and 1887. After Burgess's death in 1893, Nathanael Herreshoff rose to even greater prominence as the designer of many Cup defenders. He also designed most of the yachts and classes raced by Beverly Yacht Club members at the turn of the century and for decades beyond.

In 1898, Nat Herreshoff designed a gaff-rigged sloop called the one-design 15 footer, or the "Herreshoff 15," especially for members of the Beverly Yacht Club. The club had become discouraged by the never-ending problems of handicap racing and desired a class of one-design boats. The committee of members who commissioned the design was headed by noted yachtsman R.W. Emmons II. Eleven boats were built during the winter of 1898–1899, and they were personally delivered the following spring by Herreshoff, who towed them to

The Butler's Point clubhouse of the Beverly Yacht Club is seen here in 1913.

Marion behind his steam yacht *Squib*. Lots were drawn for these first boats and in the ensuing years, the class became very popular and approximately 70 boats were eventually built.

At Beverly Yacht Club, they were known as the E class and were commonly called Es. Today, only a few are still in existence. One of the early Es, *Fiddler*, built in 1902, was owned by Caroline M. Dabney, who in 1904 won the Beverly Yacht Club championship. In 1933, her son Augustin H. Parker and *Fiddler* won the Van Rensselaer Cup, which is given to the winner of an open handicap race that could be entered by any sailing yacht in Buzzards Bay. The Herreshoff 15 measured 24 feet 6 inches overall and 15 feet on the waterline, with a beam of 6 feet 9 inches and a draft of 2 feet 6 inches with centerboard up and 5 feet 6 inches with the board down. It was particularly well adapted to Buzzards Bay. Thirty-one of these boats had racing numbers as late as 1937 but they died out after the 1938 hurricane and World War II.

The most popular of all classes to be raced at Beverly Yacht Club has been the Herreshoff 12-and-a-half footer (commonly called Herreshoff 12), which was designed in 1914 by Nathanael Herreshoff. Measuring 12.5 feet on the waterline, 15 feet 10 inches overall, with a beam of 5 feet 10 inches and a draft of 2 feet 6

A Herreshoff 12 is under sail.

This 1880s photograph of Water Street shows the Admiral Harwood home—one of Marion's oldest houses—which eventually became the home of the Beverly Yacht Club.

inches, it was admired for its speed and responsiveness. In addition, it was a good family boat because it was comfortable, easy to sail, seaworthy, and safe. In 1915, 19 Herreshoff 12s were commissioned in Buzzards Bay for the season. By the 1930s, 300 boats were racing in Buzzards Bay with 75 racing out of Beverly in 1937.

As with all his designs, Herreshoff used a hull model instead of line drawings when designing the boat. Offsets were taken from the model and from these, mold frames were constructed to shape the hull. The boat was originally framed in oak and planked in cedar, though the familiar oak trim was changed to mahogany in 1936. The first boats sold for between $400 and $500, sails included, a figure that was considered high in those days. The Herreshoff 12 has been the most popular of all classes ever raced at the Beverly Yacht Club and was also considered the finest family boat ever developed in the opinion of most of those who sailed it.

Appearing in the 1930s, the Yankee One-Design class was the product of a designing competition and resulted in a compromise between the two best designs. The committee of yachtsmen headed by Waldo H. Brown of Boston wanted a "high, dry, and able" boat that would "stand up and take it" (be able to sail in rough conditions) in the frequently choppy and breezy waters of Buzzards Bay. At the same time, the boat had to have the speed and handling qualities that would appeal to first-rate racing skippers, and be economical to build and maintain. The first sloop was built in 1937 by Britt Bros. of Saugus, Massachusetts. It was 30 feet 6 inches long overall, 24 feet at the water line, had a 6 feet 6 inches beam and a 4 feet 6 inches draft.

Yankee One-Design class races out of Beverly Yacht Club in the late 1930s.

Sydney Herreshoff, the son of Nathanael, designed the Beverly Yacht Club dinghy, which appeared in 1951 and was popular for several short races in one day. It was also commonly used to teach tactics, rules, and trim.

From 1895 until the 1960s, the Beverly Yacht Club members also raced keel boats, dories, racing catboats, knockabouts, skimming dishes, restricted 25 footers and 18 footers, one-design Herreshoff 30s, Herreshoff 25s, Herreshoff 18s, Herreshoff K class and R class boats, Crane 15s, Cape Cod Baby knockabouts, Herreshoff Specials, M-Bs, Beetle Cats, 110s, and special classes, all of which participated in regular championship races. Members of the Beverly Yacht Club have also frequently been involved in America's Cup races, including Robert Emmons, Jack Parkinson, Chandler Hovey, and Sam Wakeman, to mention a few.

An article in the *Wareham Courier* from July 16, 1914, described one early Beverly Yacht Club race:

> The fifth race of the season was sailed under the auspices of the Beverly Yacht Club last Saturday. The yachts started in a light breeze which gradually freshened until it became a fresh wind from the southwest which made the skippers happy. Excepting the Special Class there were close contests. Perhaps the most interesting was in the Crane class when only forty-five seconds separated the first five boats at the finish. It was highly creditable to Miss Coolidge that she took first honors in this

event. The *Mirpeh* sailed well winning from the fast *Saracen* but was unable to pass the *Kaconna*. There was an exceptionally large entry in the Herreshoff class (15-Footers) and to Miss Webster went the honor of leading the fleet home. The new *Maribee* kept in the winner's column with the *Jack* and *Pronto* closely following. The 15-footers took the course to Angelica and Scraggy Neck buoys, while the others went to Nyes Ledge buoy in addition. The judge was H. Nelson Emmons.

Over the years, the Beverly Yacht Club has run many regional and national sailing events. These have included the Intercollegiates, Interscholastics, Sears Bowl, Adams Cup, and Roosevelt Bowl, in addition to special regattas. The club has also been host to J class America's Cup defenders and the famous New York 40s, and in 1956, it hosted the Olympic trials in Jolly boats and the 5.5 Meter class. In 1958, the club ran the International 110 Atlantic Coast Championships, which were dominated by a skipper of its very own—Bill Saltonstall—who borrowed a 110 at the last minute and won the championship. The club has also run International 14-foot dinghy races for the Buzzards Bay Bowl.

Since 1950, Beverly Yacht Club has sponsored the Ladies' Series, which is held every Thursday afternoon, currently in Doughdishes (fiberglass Herreshoff 12s) and Bullseyes. Beverly Yacht Club women have reached the finals of the Adams Cup, the women's national sailing championship, on three occasions. They won the Prosser Cup in 1955 and 1959 and the Colt Cup in 1955 and 1959. In 1962, a crew skippered by Wendy Peirson won the Prosser Cup, the Colt Trophy, and went to the Adams Cup finals.

In the 1960s, three new classes were added to the Beverly Yacht Club's racing schedule: Tempests, Shields, and Widgeons. The Tempest—a 22-foot, two-person keelboat designed by Ian Proctor—was adopted in the winter of 1965–1966 and ten orders were placed for the 1966 racing season. The boats were built by O'Day and the sails made by Milgram and Hopkins. The Tempest stood up well in a Buzzards Bay sou'wester and on a planing reach could take off in long bursts of speed. The class was adopted by the Olympics in 1972. In the 1960s and 1970s, the club hosted the Tempest national championships and the Atlantic championships, with 30 to 40 competitors in each hotly contested series.

The 30-foot Shields class first raced at the Beverly Yacht Club in the summer of 1968. A number of club members felt that there was a need for a larger one-design class to fill the void created by the loss of the Yankees. The classic design of the Shields delighted sailors in the fresh winds and steep chop of Buzzards Bay.

The Widgeon, a 12 feet 4 inches fiberglass center boarder with mainsail, jib, and spinnaker, came to the Beverly Yacht Club in 1968. There was need for a new boat for junior members between 12 and 16. In the first Beverly Yacht Club Junior Regatta, held in 1968, 18 out of 92 entries were Widgeons and the first three places went to club skippers. The Junior Regatta has become a major success and it is the only such event in the Southern Massachusetts Yacht Racing Association.

The following is a list of commodores of the Beverly Yacht Club:

Edward Burgess	1872–1873	J. Gordon Gibbs	1955–1956
William C. Loring	1874–1875	Lucius T. Hill	1957–1959
H.H. Buck	1876	F. Stanton Deland Jr.	1960–1962
Arthur Burgess	1877–1878	J.H. Cunningham Jr.	1963–1965
W. Lloyd Jeffries	1879–1881	William B. Cudahy	1966
Richard D. Sears	1882–1883	C.B. Converse	1967–1968
Henry Parkman	1884	Ralph Thatcher	1969–1970
Gordon Dexter	1885–1887	Richard W. Angle	1971–1972
H.M. Sears	1888	L. Hoyt Watson	1973–1975
John B. Paine	1889–1891	Roy W. Miller	1976–1978
H.P. Benson	1892–1893	David W. Johns	1979–1981
R.C. Robbins	1894–1896	W.G. Saltonstall Jr.	1982–1983
George H. Richards	1897–1902	Harvey White	1984–1985
Lewis S. Dabney	1903–1907	Thomas T. Crowley	1986–1987
W.E.C. Eustis	1908–1913	John W. Braitmayer	1988–1989
F.L. Dabney	1914–1918	Thomas H. Farquhar	1990–1991
J.L. Stackpole	1919–1925	Alan O. Stickles	1992–1993
Robert W. Cumming	1926–1939	Faith A. Paulsen	1994–1995
Henry R. Shepley	1940–1941	William S. Moonan	1996–1997
J. Lewis Stackpole	1942–1945	Graham I. Quinn	1998–1999
Donald Angier	1946–1948	John M. Buckley	2000–2001
Richard V. Wakeman	1949–1951	Henry P. Roberts	2002–present
Parker Converse	1952–1954		

The Latin inscription on the Beverly Yacht Club seal reads, *litus ama altum alii teneant*, which translates, "Others seek the deep, I like the shallow water." Since its inception, the Beverly Yacht Club has maintained a strong tradition in small boat racing. Small boats, it is said, wisely cling to the shore, but they also provide matchless sport and great experience. From its founding, Beverly Yacht Club members believed that modest sailors sailing small boats and clinging to the shore make the best deep-water sailors in the end. And while racing silverware has brought honor to the club, the love of the sea has always been more important than competition.

10. The Grand Yachts of Summer Residents

Although primarily a harbor for smaller boats, Marion has also served as the hailing port for some major yachts over the years.

Colonel Harry E. Converse's steam yacht *Parthenia*, based in Marion Harbor during the early 1900s, was designed by Nathanael Herreshoff and built by the Herreshoff Manufacturing Co. in Bristol, Rhode Island for Morton F. Plant in 1903. It was sold to Colonel Converse in 1905 and he owned her until 1919, a year before his death. *Parthenia* was 131 feet overall, drew 5.5 feet of water, with a beam of 18 feet 4 inches. While a steam yacht, she also sported two raked masts and sails: the after mast 90 feet, gaff rigged; and the forward mast 70 feet, square rigged. She reportedly could make 12 knots under steam and sail and 10 knots under steam alone. *Parthenia* had a teak double-planked hull with bulb angle-iron frame and teak decks. Although she was a rugged craft, she also had six staterooms with accommodations for 15, a galley, library, music room, main dining salon, and living salon. The anchor windlass was electric, and there was instant hot water in all parts of the yacht.

Colonel Converse was a leader in the American rubber industry, and he and his family were among the earliest wealthy families to make their summer home in Marion. Mary Parker Converse, the colonel's wife, was probably the first and only woman of her time to become a licensed sea captain. She served, after her husband's death, as a navigator aboard a freighter. During World War II, she obtained a master's rating in the U.S. Merchant Marine and taught navigation to naval recruits. In addition to all this, she wrote papers for scientific journals and published a book entitled *113 Days on Iron Decks*. Mary Parker Converse died at age 89. Relatives of Colonel Converse and his family still live in Marion today.

In 1926, Cox & Stephens designed and Newport News Shipbuilding constructed *Arcadia*, one of the first private yachts to be diesel powered. She was built for Galen Luther Stone, though he was able to use the yacht only once before his death in December 1926. Born in 1862, Stone founded Hayden, Stone & Company in 1892 with Charles Hayden. The firm prospered and by 1922 had

Colonel Converse's Parthenia *leaves Sippican Harbor for a day cruise, c. 1905.*

$30 million in capital. In 1889 Stone married Carrie Morton Gregg and the couple had four children: Katharine, Margaret ("Peggy"), Barbara, and Robert.

Stone's daughter Peggy (Mrs. Huntington Reed Hardwick) inherited *Arcadia* and cruised extensively with her from 1927 to 1939. Galen Stone had required a yacht sufficiently large to be used as a summer home for himself and his family, but he also felt that it was essential the yacht be an excellent sea boat, suited for extended offshore voyages. *Arcadia* was 188 feet long, with a beam of 27 feet 6 inches and a draft of 11 feet. She had an excellent seagoing steel hull and two Winton diesel engines, which were 800 horsepower each. There were also two diesel-driven electric generators of 35 kilowatts each, diesel- and electric-driven air compressors, a large electric-operated refrigerating plant, a hot water heating plant with radiators in all the living spaces, and a forced ventilating system operated by electricity. *Arcadia* had a maximum speed of 16 knots and her fuel oil tanks provided sufficient capacity for a cruise of 9,000 miles. She had staterooms for 12 and required a crew of 23. There were also quarters for use by pilots and fishing guides. She carried five small boats, all made of cedar, teak trimmed, and painted white: a 33-foot owner's speed launch, a 26-foot owner's regular launch, a 21-foot crew's launch, a 20-foot lifeboat, and a 14-foot dinghy. During World War II, *Arcadia* was converted into a Canadian escort vessel. After the war she became a ferry and was reportedly scrapped in 1969.

Marilee, one of the New York 40s designed by Nathanael Herreshoff and built by the Herreshoff Manufacturing Co. for members of the New York Yacht Club (Morgan, Bell, Kellogg, and Coolidge, to name a few), was built in 1926 for Edward I. Cudahy, a publisher from the Midwest who summered in Marion. He commissioned Herreshoff to build him a yacht so that his wife, Marilee, an avid sailor, and young son William could sail.

The yacht was 59 feet overall, 40 feet on the waterline, and her beam was 14 feet 3 inches. She carried 2,426 square feet of sail. This one-design racing boat was the second-to-last of the class to be built. In 1916, a dozen of these boats were launched from the Herreshoff Manufacturing Co. in Bristol and were considered by some to be the hottest racing class of their time. They were rugged boats that were able to embrace heavy weather. They were known as the "Fighting Forties" or the "Roaring Forties" because of the intensity of their racing. Two 40s, *Memory* in 1924 and *Rugosa II* in 1928, won the prestigious Newport-to-Bermuda Race. Marilee Cudahy died of cancer in the mid-1930s and a heartbroken Edward Cudahy sold *Marilee* shortly thereafter. The boat was recently restored by a syndicate from the New York Yacht Club for the 150th anniversary of the America's Cup in Cowes, England, in August 2001.

Nashira, an 81-foot power yacht built in 1924, was the first of the high-speed, houseboat-type commuters developed by Consolidated Shipbuilders of New York City. She was one of five boats of her type that were meant to combine the comforts of a houseboat with the speed of a commuter. Built for Richard F. Hoyt of New York and Marion, *Nashira* had an enclosed pilothouse forward followed by a large saloon. She had a good-sized afterdeck and cockpit along with three staterooms below and plenty of light and ventilation. *Nashira* was a comfortable vessel and was fast for such a large package. Powered by two 500-horsepower

Galen L. Stone's Arcadia, *a 188-foot diesel yacht, was built in 1926.*

Marilee *is pictured here at the start of the New York 40 New York Yacht Club Cruise in 1926.*

Wright Typhoon V-12s, she stepped out at almost 30 miles per hour. This was as good as many of the smaller and lighter express cruisers of the Jazz Age.

But Richard Hoyt's serious high-speed commuter yacht was *Teaser*, a famous George Crouch design built by Nevins and powered by a single Wright Typhoon V-12 that made better than 50 miles per hour. In 1925, the 39-foot 10-inch *Teaser* ran up the Hudson from New York City to Albany at 52 miles per hour to beat the time of the Twentieth Century Limited express train by 27 minutes. Although a bona fide commuter, *Teaser* was essentially a speedboat. Hoyt also owned *Vamoose*, a 61-foot motor yacht built in 1914.

Cecelia J (later *Dorothy G*), designed by Walter McInnis of the Boston naval architectural firm Eldredge-McInnis, Inc., was an 82-foot auxiliary schooner whose name changed from the first wife to the second when the owner divorced and remarried. This large and distinctive schooner was built by Quincy Adams in 1956 for the rich and somewhat eccentric Joseph H. Plumb Jr., who commissioned the vessel to take him in safety and style to Iceland, which was about to celebrate the 1,000th anniversary of its parliament.

The vessel was a modified Gloucester fisherman that was eminently fit to take the worst punishment a winter gale in the North Atlantic could hand her—and to take this punishment while her owner's party and crew enjoyed below-deck comforts never dreamed of on a Banks schooner. It had princely accommodations for a large professional crew of four (skipper, mate, engineer, and cook) and an owner's party of five—it was a cruising boat that put safety and comfort before all other considerations. Performance under power exceeded expectations with her General Motors 6-71 diesel (165 horsepower) and a 4.5:1 reduction gear swinging a five-bladed propeller. She made better than 10 knots at 1,650 r.p.m. Her equipment included Dacron sails by Manchester, a U.S. Motors generator, Way-Wolff ship heater, Ideal windlass, Crowell water pressure system, and a Rudd hot water heater. She had a 110-volt system using Bowers batteries and carried a deep freeze and refrigerator. Hooked up to her Edson steering gear was a Sperry automatic pilot. She had Morse controls, Raytheon radar and Fathometer, Sperry loran and an RCA radiotelephone. She carried 1,062 gallons of fuel in steel tanks and 745 gallons of water in Monel tanks. She had an oak backbone and sawn frames, 2.25-inch mahogany planking, teak deck and trim, and galvanized iron and bronze fastenings. Merriman Bros., Nevins, and the Quincy Adams Yacht Yard furnished her hardware. She was equipped with electric sheet and halyard winches engineered to make a big vessel manageable by two or three men under any and all conditions.

Below deck were thousands of dollars' worth of specially engraved silverware, monogrammed white goods, and decorated crockery. (When *Cecelia J* became the *Dorothy G*, all this had to go.) From boot top to railcap, the schooner was painted in commercial fisherman style—dark green topsides with white bulwarks and housesides—but the elaborate gilt scrollwork and cove stripe and the varnished spars and other bright work were additions not to be found in commercial fishing boats but rather in pleasure boats. Plumb trusted Captain Roy Miller with the entire management of the vessel.

Walter McInnis also designed a 25-foot Friendship sloop for Joseph Plumb Jr. for use as a daysailer. Built by Simms Brothers of Dorchester, the *Dotty G* was at the time probably the most expensive wooden boat of her length ever built, as well

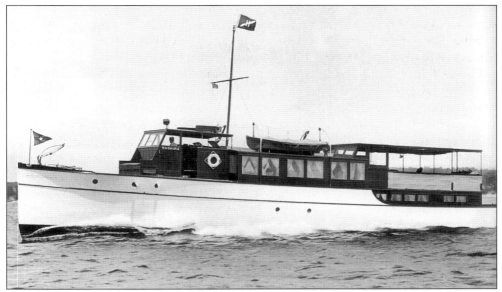

Nashira *flies owner Richard F. Hoyt's private signal and the New York Yacht Club burgee.*

as probably the most perfectly finished Friendship sloop. *Dotty G*'s counter was carved in conformity with that of *Dorothy G*, and both boats were identically painted. When they lay in a slip side by side, the *Dotty G*'s exquisite Tamm-built dinghy tied up astern made everyone appreciate such beauty. After Joseph Plumb's death, *Dorothy G/Cecelia J* was sold to a Dutch yachtsman from The Hague, who in turn sold her to Prince Rainier of Monaco.

Harry E. Converse, Galen L. Stone, Edward I. Cudahy, Richard F. Hoyt, and Joseph H. Plumb Jr. chose Marion for their summer homes because of its excellent winds and cruising grounds, and they brought their grand yachts with them.

Cecelia J/Dorothy G, under 3,700 square feet of sail, goes on a shakedown cruise in the spring of 1956.

11. SEASIDE RESORT

Following the Civil War and the post–Civil War boom in tourism, the forgotten seaport of Marion experienced a rebirth. The New York, New Haven & Hartford Railroad made Marion more accessible from Boston, New York, Philadelphia, Washington, and other cities throughout the country. The influx of wealthy summer visitors to Marion in the late nineteenth century led to the town's "Gilded Age" because of the writers, artists, politicians, and philanthropists who brought cultural and material wealth to this small coastal town.

It all began when Richard Watson Gilder, the editor of *Century Magazine*, came to Marion in the 1880s at the urging of his childhood friend Bessy Harwood, who thought that Gilder needed a respite from the heat and stresses of New York City. She wrote of Marion to him, saying, "Its toneless air would administer to perfect rest." Bessy was the daughter of retired Civil War Admiral Andrew Harwood, who summered in Marion in the home that houses the present Beverly Yacht Club. Admiral Harwood also founded Saint Gabriel's Episcopal Church in Marion.

Once Gilder arrived, he purchased an old abandoned stone building that was once used for the storage of salt and converted it into a studio for his artist wife, Helena deKay Gilder. The Gilders' friend Stanford White of the architecture firm McKim, Mead and White designed a new fireplace for the "Old Stone Studio" (which still stands today). It was there that the Gilders hosted a salon for all of their illustrious friends.

Celebrities who came at the invitation of the Gilders included artist-illustrator Charles Dana Gibson (creator of the "Gibson Girl"), sculptor Augustus St. Gaudens, actresses Ethel Barrymore, Maude Adams, and Evelyn Nesbitt, and actors John Drew and John Barrymore. Other friends of the Gilders included Louis Agassiz, the great naturalist; Frank Stockton, writer of "The Lady or the Tiger"; John C. Nicolay and John Hay, Lincoln biographers; and Joe Jefferson, the beloved actor who made a career out of playing Rip Van Winkle and who was a steady fishing companion of Grover Cleveland. The writer Henry James was also a friend of Gilder and visited him in Marion. In his 1866 novel *The Bostonians*, James brought his hero to Marion. The town described by James in the book was still in decline before it became nationally famous. He describes a straggling, loosely clustered town beside a blue inlet "whose houses looked at each other

The Sippican Hotel and Casino are seen from the harbor late in the nineteenth century.

across the grass—low, rusty, crooked, distended houses with dry, cracked faces and dim rays of small-paned, stiffly sliding windows. Their little dooryard bristled with rank, old-fashioned flowers, mostly yellow." He further wrote, "Old men sat in their doorways, old captains, many of them men with faces like lost battles, living in the past. . . . Shipyards were silent; the whalers were almost gone from the sea. Many widows of sailors wrecked in distant parts of the oceans were living in the old houses. Many widows and mothers of boys lost in the Civil War sat in the church pews on Sundays."

Gilder, a poet and one of the best known editors in the United States, changed all that. He did not look like the forerunner of Marion's golden age when he walked down the streets in a flowing blue cape and wide hat. He was a small man, and the townsfolk thought he looked a little like Edgar Allan Poe. His adversaries described him as a "long-haired weakling," "tender apple blossom," and a "quivering mouse." But he was a very powerful man and filled his magazine with hard-hitting crusades against the evils of his time. He fought against New York City's crumbling tenements and their wealthy owners and even took on New York's Trinity Church tenements. Trinity Church, a house of worship for New York's most wealthy and socially prominent citizens, subsequently issued its first financial statement in 100 years and began to improve the tenements it owned. Walt Whitman said of Gilder, "When most everybody else in their set threw me down, the Gilders were nobly and unhesitatingly hospitable . . . and took me in."

Gilder also invited President Grover Cleveland and family to Marion to escape the hot Washington summers. Gilder and President Cleveland first became friends when Cleveland was governor of New York and Gilder played a major role in Cleveland's winning of the White House. Frances Cleveland, the young wife of the president, first visited Marion during the summer of 1887 and stayed with noted Arctic explorer Adolphus Greeley. The Clevelands spent four summers in Marion between his first (1885–1889) and second (1893–1897) terms as president. Frances Cleveland took part in many Marion activities. She was charming and without pretense and often walked the village streets alone, talking with children and old men on the piers. The Clevelands, who loved Marion so much they named one of their daughters after the town, tried to purchase the house they rented on Harbor Lane (now 46 Water Street), but the owners named too high a price and the Clevelands purchased another home in Bourne, Massachusetts, instead.

At the turn of the twentieth century, Marion had two grand hotels in which the summer visitors stayed: the Marion House at Great Hill and the Sippican Hotel and Casino on Harbor Lane (now called Water Street). Harbor Lane, which ran along the bay in the village, began to sport grand shingle-style summer homes (which they called "cottages") during this period. Not only did President and Mrs. Cleveland live on Harbor Lane, but also the Davises from Philadelphia and the Clarks from Chicago.

Richard Harding Davis was the most famous war correspondent at the turn of the century and he married Cecil Clark Davis in the chapel of Saint Gabriel's Church in 1899. Ethel Barrymore was maid of honor and Charles Dana Gibson was in the wedding party. Newspapermen flocked to Marion to record the gala event, which became front-page news across the country. Cecil traveled with Richard after the wedding while he covered the Boer War, and over the years they traveled together, sharing hardships, adventures, and wars around the world. After

Richard Harding Davis and his wife, Cecil Clark Davis, enjoy Sippican Harbor.

10 years of marriage, Cecil filed for divorce, an almost unthinkable action at the time. In her suit, she cited Bessie McCoy (a Broadway chorus girl referred to as the "Yamma Yamma Girl") by name, and once the divorce was final, Richard Harding Davis married McCoy. The couple had a daughter and remained together until Richard died of a heart attack in 1916. Cecil, who had once studied painting with John Singer Sargent, one of America's great portrait painters, continued to live in Marion where many famous people sat for her portraits. Roald Amundsen and Charles Lindberg were two of her subjects. Lindberg came to Marion when his son attended Tabor's summer camp.

Many other famous people came to Marion. Architect Henry Hobson Richardson not only visited Marion, but the smallest house he ever designed is located here. It all started out as a bet. Richardson's friend the Reverend Percy Browne bet Richardson, whose best known work is probably the Trinity Church in Boston, that he could not design a house to be built for $2,500. Richardson won the bet when he designed a shingle-style home in 1881 overlooking the bay as a "country house" for Reverend Browne. It still stands at 192 Front Street.

Admiral William S. Sims lived in East Marion on Sippican Neck. He is credited with doing more to improve ship design, fleet tactics, and naval gunnery than any other man in U.S. naval history. During World War I, he commanded all U.S. Navy forces in Europe and promoted the convoy system, which helped defeat the German U-boat menace. Musician Walter Damrosch and Episcopal Bishop of Massachusetts Phillips Brooks also came to visit the Gilders. Bishop Brooks was also known for writing the Christmas carol "O Little Town of Bethlehem."

President Franklin Delano Roosevelt, left, swims with his friend and physician Dr. William McDonald in Marion's waters.

Dr. McDonald of Marion and President Roosevelt enjoy a day on the water.

President Franklin Delano Roosevelt came to Marion to be treated by his friend and physician Dr. William McDonald for his infantile paralysis. Roosevelt stayed at McDonald's home on Main Street and would climb the stairs in Dr. McDonald's house every day. When Roosevelt founded the health resort Warm Springs in Georgia, he made use of Dr. McDonald's ideas.

Colonel Harry E. Converse, an heir of Elisha Converse, the founder of a rubber products industry in Malden, Massachusetts, during the 1850s and whose rubber shoes were in great demand worldwide, came to Marion in 1890 and built an estate called the "Moorings" at the tip of Converse Point. Converse was an important philanthropist who funded many local causes including Marion's fire department. In 1907, Galen Stone, a Boston investment banker who founded Hayden Stone, purchased Great Hill, site of the grand old summer hotel Marion House. Stone demolished the hotel and built a rambling stone mansion in the style of a Tudor manor house north of London called Compton Wyngates. By 1911, the Stones had moved into the massive summer "castle" with 30 servants. Another 20 male employees lived in a separate staff building on the grounds. Reduced in size by approximately four-fifths today, the residence is still a substantial stone and brick edifice.

Today, Marion's population almost doubles in the summer when the "summer folk" return each year to enjoy the warm breezes, cruising, yacht racing, fishing, swimming, and all the happy gatherings. Marion is still a place to "get away from it all" and a place to enjoy life's gifts. It is a special place where happiness abounds.

12. Maritime Industry in the Twentieth Century

Marion's seaside location has continued to foster maritime industries in the twentieth and now the twenty-first centuries. In the early twentieth century, it was Marion's location that caused the Marconi Wireless Telegraph Company to choose the town for one of its stations. The Sippican Corporation began in 1958 providing fabrication services to Francis Associates, a Marion partnership. Today, Sippican is a successful high-tech employer of many Marion residents.

Marconi Wireless Telegraph Company

On December 12, 1901, Guglielmo Marconi, an Italian electrical engineer who made the basic discoveries that led to wireless telegraphy, was the first man to send a transatlantic wireless signal. He later received the Nobel Prize in physics for developing his wave system of long-distance communication.

In 1914, Marion was chosen as the site of the largest and most powerful wireless telegraph station in the world. The Marion station was one of 11 built around the world by the Marconi Wireless Telegraph Company, a pioneer in wireless communications. Its purpose was to communicate directly with a high-powered wireless plant in Stavanger, Norway. Marion was selected because of its latitude and longitude in relation to the Norwegian station and also because it was close enough to the ocean to allow overseas transmissions, but far enough away—it was thought—that it would be safe during hurricanes.

The Marconi Company purchased 143 acres of land west of the railroad station in Marion and along the tracks of the New York, New Haven & Hartford Railroad. The land was composed of several parcels owned by the Hiller brothers, W.H.H. Ryder, Captain George D. Allen, the heirs of W.E. Sparrow, and the heirs of Barnabas Holmes. At the time the Marion station was built, high-power stations varied from 2 to 25 kilowatts output, with the greatest power supplied at 75 kilowatts. The actual transmitting energy of the Marion station was 300 kilowatts. The January 29, 1914 *Wareham Courier* reported that wireless telegraphy was "one of the wonders of the twentieth century and it is gratifying to know that the most powerful station thus far designed is to be erected in this vicinity."

The station consisted of 14 towers, each 408 feet high, that extended parallel to the railroad for a mile. It was built to handle all trans-Atlantic radio traffic. When finished, it had the effect of a one-third reduction in the rates charged for messages. The Marion station was the sending station, and the receiving station was at Chatham, 40 miles away. The Chatham station received mainly marine messages and transmitted them to Marion via two telegraph lines. By separating the stations, the company avoided static difficulties, which occurred when the same aerials were used for sending and receiving.

The Marion station was to be manned around the clock, so the company erected a brick home for the superintendent and a brick hotel to house 18 men in addition to an operating building. The first superintendent was M.T. Rossi.

But World War I interfered with the business plans of the Marconi Company when the U.S. government determined that communications should not be in foreign hands. The Navy assumed control of all of Marconi's stations in the United States for the duration of World War I, and it was not until 1919 that the station was brought into operation and the first trial message sent across the ocean to Norway. At the end of the war, the Radio Corporation of America (RCA) acquired all the Marconi properties in the United States.

On June 27, 1920, the *New Bedford Sunday Standard* reported on the Marion Marconi Station, which was now owned by RCA: "Flashing straight as a die across three thousand miles of rolling ocean, wireless messages from the mammoth

Workers build Marion's Marconi towers in 1914.

station at Marion are now sounding in the ear of the distant operator at Stavanger, Norway. Communication is nearly continuous night and day." The same author explained to his readers, "A wireless message may be likened to a pebble thrown into a smooth pond. Where the stone strikes the surface, ripples spread in circles. The ripple and the wireless wave are the same, the wave occurring by an instrument in the station and circling out broadcast, and growing weaker and weaker as it spreads from its starting point."

The 1920s were the heyday of the Marion station which, in addition to other duties, broadcasted the weather to ships at sea. Marion ended up with four short-wave channels, one intermediate-wave, and two long-wave. During World War II, the Marion station was used by the Army Air Force when communications once again became of vital interest to the nation. The station communicated with undersea craft and with planes flying near Arctic zones.

Marion broadcasted to many points of the globe, contacting both sea-going vessels and airships. Some of its more famous contacts were to Admiral Richard E. Byrd on his trips to Little America in Antarctica, to Colonel and Mrs. Charles Lindbergh over the Atlantic Ocean and Europe, and to the *Graf Zeppelin* during regular trips between Berlin and South American ports.

In 1947, the Marion wireless station closed, and in 1949, RCA leased the land to the U.S. Air Force. The Air Force purchased all of the station's equipment, and its Airways and Air Communications Service (AACS) ran the 200,000-watt

A close-up photograph shows the base of a Marconi tower.

This is one of the 14 Marconi towers that rose 440 feet over Marion.

station. AACS had the responsibility for controlling, operating, and maintaining all air navigational aids for all air services, including radio-range stations, homing beacons, control towers, and blind-control landing equipment. For AACS, the station provided a central point for the clearing of communications to the Air Force's outlying air bases, reaching out to North Atlantic stations, Iceland, Newfoundland, Greenland, and Western Europe. Communications also went to the Azores and as far south as the Caribbean Air Command. The AACS gathered weather information throughout the world for the Air Weather Service for use in forecasting weather conditions on all air routes.

In 1956, the Marion AACS station was shut down. With the introduction of new satellite-based methods of weather transmission, it had become obsolete. In 1960, 13 towers were taken down because they had begun to deteriorate. Later that year, RCA sold the property to Elden M. Love, the owner of the Marion Lumber Company, for $78,100.79. It was estimated that the remaining scrap was worth $10,000. One of the station's two alternators is now in the Smithsonian Museum in Washington, D.C.

The Marion Marconi station had long been a landmark because of its antennas, which were visible for miles. For a time a 30-inch-diameter red beam on one of the masts cast its light at least 20 miles. One tower remains at the site today as a reminder of a time gone by. It is still used by a local cable company, which attaches microwave dishes to the tower to receive signals beamed from satellites.

Sippican Corporation founders Van Clark and Tim Francis are pictured here.

SIPPICAN, INC.

The Sippican Corporation is a Marion company that capitalized on the community's seaside location. Thayer Francis, a resident of Marion, founded Francis Associates in 1946 as a small consulting engineering firm. In its early years the company provided facilities design work for architectural firms, and later on provided specialized studies and design services for military installations and industrial facilities.

In 1958, the concept of three-dimensional electronic subassemblies was developed by Francis Associates. Sam Francis discovered that when electronic components were tightly compacted and the circuit board eliminated, i.e., made smaller and lighter with no empty spaces, the assembly became more reliable. The successful application of this technique (known as high-density electronics packaging) led to the formation of a separate electronics design operation at Francis Associates and to the 1958 incorporation of Sippican, which was to provide fabrication services to Francis Associates.

The founders of Sippican were W. Van Allen Clark Jr., assistant dean of the Sloan School at the Massachusetts Institute of Technology and a Marion resident, and three partners from Francis Associates: Samuel A. Francis, Thayer Francis Jr., and Phillip Taber. Van Clark provided the seed money, Sam Francis was the inventor, Phil Taber was in charge of manufacturing, and Tim Francis provided marketing and general management. Van Clark eventually became chairman; Tim Francis, president; and Sam Francis and Phil Taber became vice presidents of Marion's newly formed Sippican Corporation.

In 1964, Sippican developed the Expendable Bathythermograph System (XBT) probe for the oceanographic market. A temperature measuring instrument key to the use of sonar, the XBT system facilitated increases in knowledge and interpretation of the ocean environment. The XBT proved a significant advance in tactical anti-submarine warfare operations, as well as for research and commercial uses—some even liked to claim that it translated the "secrets of the sea." The Sippican annual report for 1968 stated that the XBT system was being operated from 280 naval, research, and commercial vessels.

The Sippican XBT was expendable, which meant that it was utilized as a "one-shot device" to gather temperature and depth information. The U.S. Navy purchased the probe because it was proven to have the greatest accuracy, the deepest depth capability, the greatest ship speed, the highest reliability, and the lowest per-unit cost. The Navy ordered an initial production quantity along with the associated launchers and recorders. Other navies followed, and by the early 1970s, virtually every Allied naval vessel was deploying XBTs. Oceanographers also used XBTs from research vessels to collect and share ocean thermal data.

Sippican continued to develop, adapt, and integrate sensors for its products. These included other expendables that measured sound velocity, current velocity, electrical conductivity, optical irradiance, and sediment characterization for deployment from surface ship-, submarine-, and aircraft-launched profilers.

The success of the submarine-launched XBT system brought about the formation of the Oceanographic Systems Division of Sippican in 1966 and the concentration of engineering ability in a variety of instrumentation problems confronting the oceanographic community. Also in 1966, Sippican became the parent company and Francis Associates, Inc. became a wholly owned subsidiary. By 1968, the company had grown from 6 employees in 1946 to more than 500 with annual sales of $10 million. In 1970, Sippican celebrated the production of its 500,000th XBT probe for the Navy.

Sippican executives hold the millionth XBT unit in 1972.

In 1972, the company celebrated the manufacture of its millionth probe, noting the worldwide distribution of its XBT equipment. It had manufacturing licensees in the United Kingdom, Japan, and France, and had distributors covering more than 50 percent of free nations. More than six million XBTs have been produced.

The company has developed three divisions for its current business operations: Sea-Air Systems, Underwater Vehicles, and Countermeasure Systems. The Sea-Air Systems division's products include expendable probes like the XBT, as well as probes that measure atmospheric conditions such as temperature, winds, and humidity. This division also manufactures launching devices and data acquisition systems, which record, process, and interpret the data the probes collect.

The Underwater Vehicles division produces an underwater mobile acoustic target used in anti-submarine warfare training by the U.S. Navy and other free-world navies. The Countermeasure Systems division has developed a missile defense decoy for the U.S. Navy in a joint program with the Australian Navy. It supplies expendable cartridges for ship-borne chaff, infrared and acoustic decoys, decoy launchers and launch systems, and related training and tactic development systems to the U.S. Navy and international military customers.

Today, Sippican, Inc. continues its work in ocean science and engineering and in developing and producing sensors and instrumentation systems to support Navy undersea warfare requirements and other government-funded endeavors and programs. In 2000, Sippican's revenues were in excess of $70 million. Marion's maritime industries have progressed greatly over the years and are currently regarded as state of the art due to the efforts of Sippican.

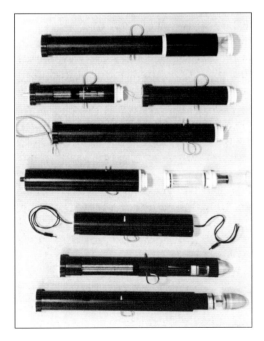

At left are several types of Sippican Expendable Wire Links (XWL). The basic components of an XWL include one or two spools of very fine conductor wire. The wire can be de-reeled from the spools at speeds up to 80 knots while conducting DC or audio signals. It also has a special insulation allowing the use of lengths of 30,000 feet or more in sea water.

13. TABOR ACADEMY

Tabor Academy was founded in 1876 by Elizabeth Taber, Marion's town benefactress. The school originally provided a free secondary education for Marion children and was the first institution of higher learning in southeastern Massachusetts. But the school languished until 1916, when, at age 35, the assistant headmaster of Phillips Andover Academy, Walter Huston Lillard, took over as the fifth headmaster of Tabor Academy. Lillard stayed at Tabor until 1942 and was responsible for reviving a "dead academy." He recognized that Tabor's location by the sea was unique and began to capitalize on that fact to attract and retain students.

The first move Lillard made at Tabor was to replace all the school's teachers and turn the institution into a boy's boarding school by removing all the town girls to a different building. The school no longer accepted boarding girls after 1916. Lillard cancelled plans to make the school the town of Marion's public school and was determined to keep the privately endowed facility independent.

The new headmaster recognized that the beautiful harbor was an invaluable asset to the school. He began to use it for training and sports for Tabor's students. He also selected a new seal for Tabor Academy. It pictured a full-rigged ship prepared to sail toward broader horizons, the years 1876 and 1916 commemorating the founding and re-organization of the school, and the motto "All-a-taut-o," which is a nautical term meaning "Everything shipshape and ready to run." Lillard made use of the harbor for the first time when he began sailing, rowing, and swimming programs at the school, stating that his goal was to build character in boys by use of the sea.

Lillard felt that a boy who could master a small boat would gain feelings of independence and confidence at a young age. In addition, he felt that rowing and deep-water sailing encouraged teamwork. The headmaster also required all students to wear naval uniforms once the waterfront program got underway because he felt that it helped to unify the student body.

Lillard moved the school from Spring Street to the waterfront so that the students would be closer to the deep-water cruising program, small boat sailing, and crew activities. He began offering spring recess cruises to the Caribbean and Central America. In 1917, Lillard asked the U.S. Navy for the loan of two 31-foot

The schooner Black Duck *was on loan to Tabor Academy from 1918 to 1925.*

cutters for the school's nautical program. Lillard also began Camp Cleveland (named after summer resident Grover Cleveland), a six-week training program and independent adjunct to the Junior Naval Reserve. The camp provided rudimentary naval training to 120 boys who were expecting to enter the armed forces. The boys trained in cutter drill, small boat sailing, knots, signaling, wireless telegraphy, infantry drill, rifle practice, wrestling, and hiking. Admiral Francis T. Bowles was chairman of the camp's advisory committee.

Lillard also asked Alexander Forbes if Tabor might use his schooner *Black Duck* for a summer deep-water cruising program, a request Forbes honored for seven summers until 1924. *Black Duck*, a 68-foot schooner built in 1909 in East Boothbay, Maine, contained ten bunks. Fostering the maritime tradition of the school, it took boys out on extended cruises. These cruises were so successful that in 1925 a committee was formed at the school called "The Tabor Boy Trust," which raised $14,000 by the sale of no-interest bonds to purchase another boat.

The committee located an 88-foot schooner in Camden, Maine, called *Robin*, which it purchased for the school. The ship was built of wood in 1902 at City Island, New York, and could accommodate 26 people. Renamed *Tabor Boy*, the boat cruised between Canada and the Chesapeake Bay. Its total sail area was 5,372 square feet and it had a 68-horsepower engine. The purchase of this schooner marked the beginning of Tabor Academy's distinctive sailing program, unmatched by that of any other secondary school in the country. The vessel carried the school's name up and down the East Coast as well as up the Hudson River and through the Great Lakes to the Chicago World's Fair in 1933.

To further the nautical image of Tabor Academy, a clock was installed in the belfry atop Lillard Hall in 1927. It was dedicated by Silas Howland in the presence of his father, Clark P. Howland, Tabor's first headmaster. At the time, the clock was one of only three of its size to strike the hours in ship's bells. Only the Portsmouth Navy Yard and the U.S. Naval Academy had similar clocks in 1927.

The Tabor Academy today has the distinction of being one of only two Honor Naval Schools in the United States and that status allows the school to nominate graduates to the United States Service Academies. Beginning in 1917, when Camp Cleveland was set up as an independent adjunct of the Junior Naval Reserve, Tabor Academy developed a growing naval tradition. On November 27, 1941, Tabor received official recognition from the U.S. Navy for the school's work with its students in seamanship and navigation.

In 1928, Headmaster Lillard hired Lieutenant James A. Lewis, USNR, to organize a full-time nautical training program on the water in the summer and teach in the classroom in the winter. At Tabor, he was given the title of "Captain" of the *Tabor Boy*. Captain Lewis taught mathematics, chemistry, history, and naval science, and the cruising program was converted into a naval training course.

The original Tabor Boy *was in service from 1925 to 1945.*

The yawl Tabor Boy II *(formerly* Edlu II*) was in service from 1945 to 1954.*

By 1930, the school had a formal nautical training program consisting of the care and use of small boats under power, sail, and oar; racing and racing tactics; seamanship; sailing rules of the road; and navigation. *Tabor Boy* was in use at the school from 1925 to 1945.

The yawl *Tabor Boy II*, formerly *Edlu II*, was acquired by the school in 1945 and was in service until 1954. Built at City Island, New York, the boat was lent by her owner Rudolph Schaefer in 1942 to the U.S. Coast Guard as a Coast Guard Auxiliary vessel for use in submarine detection off the East Coast. It cost $100,000 and was designed especially for the Newport-to-Bermuda races, which Schaefer won in 1934. The yawl was 68 feet 5 inches long overall, 48 feet long on the waterline, 14 feet 8 inches in beam, and 9 feet 3 inches in draft, with a sail area of 2,125 square feet. Tabor students entered the Bermuda Races of 1950 and 1952 with this yawl.

In 1954, the schooner *Bestevaer*, a former Dutch North Sea Pilot Schooner and the next *Tabor Boy*, was presented to the school by Ralph C. Allen of Grand Rapids, Michigan, and South Carolina. Originally built in Amsterdam in 1914, she was 92 feet in overall length, with a total sail area in excess of 6,800 square feet. The schooner was used as *Pilot Schooner #2* off the Netherlands coast until 1923, when all Dutch sailing pilot vessels were retired for steam vessels. Allen purchased the schooner in 1952 in Amsterdam, and in 1953, she was sailed to Wadmalaw Island, South Carolina. The *SSV Tabor Boy* is still in use at Tabor Academy today not only for its cruising programs, but also for its Orientation at Sea and Coral Reef Ecology programs.

Being at the edge of the sea also put the school at risk during the hurricanes of 1938, 1944, 1954, 1985, and 1991. The 1938 hurricane caused 500 casualties in New England. *Tabor Boy* survived the massive destruction because Captain James A. Lewis and Henry Barnes, the school engineer, were on board riding on full scope to three anchors. Despite snapping two cables and dragging her third anchor 150 yards, she was almost alone in surviving in the harbor. Normal high tide increased 10 feet and Lillard Hall found 5 to 6 feet of muddy water in its living and dining rooms. Tabor suffered approximately $25,000 in damage, one-fourth of the school's total income, forcing it into debt and postponing further building programs. The 1954 hurricane caused $93,000 in damage, and after that, the school decided to expand inland across Front Street to higher ground.

Tabor Academy also excelled in its crew program. Miss Edith Austin of Marion donated the first rowing shell to Tabor Academy and she continued to donate shells as the sport grew at Tabor. In 1922, Roderick Beebe came to Tabor Academy to coach crew after he had rowed at Yale and coached at Camp Pasquaney.

The 1930s certainly began the golden age of crew at Tabor. In 1931, Tabor Academy went to the prestigious Henley Regatta in England. Because the team

The schooner SSV Tabor Boy *(formerly* Bestevaer*) was in service from 1954 to the present. The vessel now serves as a floating classroom for Orientation at Sea and other programs.*

had trained on the rough waters of Sippican Harbor, they found the water conditions on the Thames very favorable. In 1932, the Tabor crew team was one of only two American entries, the other being the Harvard third crew. Tabor won the regatta in 1936, 1937, and 1939 (for an unprecedented third time) and took the cup home to Marion. The Henley Regattas were suspended between the years 1940 and 1947 because of World War II. In 1947, Tabor lost to Kent in the final, and in 1952—Tabor's eighth time at Henley—the school lost in the final to the London Club "nearly stopped by a crab," which means that one of the rower's oars got stuck under the water causing the boat to stop in the water.

The 1957 Tabor yearbook featured a tribute to Tabor's crew coach: "Perhaps crew is the best known of all Tabor sports. Tabor crews have participated in numerous Henley regattas in England in the past years and in the New England Interscholastic Rowing Championship every year. The over-all record of wins in these races is very creditable and is due, in large part, to the excellent coaching of Mr. Beebe."

In 1965 the Tabor varsity crew again went to England's Henley Regatta and won the Princess Elizabeth Cup. Two Marion boys, Wiley Wakeman and Robert

Tabor's 1939 Henley crew posed with its shell before boarding the Queen Mary *for the passage to England and winning the championship for an unprecedented third time.*

Tabor, on the left, rows against Yale at Henley on July 5, 1934. Because Tabor trained on the rough waters of Sippican Harbor, they found the conditions on the Thames favorable.

Cunningham, were on the winning team. In 1967, Tabor finished second at the Henley Regatta. In recent years the boy's crew team was the undefeated New England Champion in 1997 and competed at the Royal Henley Regatta in England in 1987, 1989, 1991, 1994, and 1999.

Spring vacation at Tabor Academy means the Spring Cruising Program, which began in 1919. Headmaster Lillard believed that the cause of international peace could be furthered by schoolboy contacts. He also hoped to expose his Tabor boys to foreign travel experiences. In 1919, the first spring cruise was taken on a United Fruit Company boat to Cuba, Panama, and Costa Rica. In 1927, Tabor students went to Panama, Guatemala, Havana, and Kingston; in 1928, to Guatemala, Honduras, and Puerto Rico; in 1929, to the Dominican Republic, Mexico, Guatemala, and Honduras; and in 1932, two cruises went to Panama, two to Columbia, one to Mexico, and one to Puerto Rico.

The 1958 Tabor yearbook discussed the weekend cruises on the *Tabor Boy* as follows: "This year over two thousand miles were logged by the schooner on her week-end cruises. Included in her itinerary were such ports of call as Boston, Gloucester, and Scituate, Massachusetts and Mystic, Connecticut." The 1959 yearbook also highlighted the activities of the *Tabor Boy*:

> The first cruise of the year was to Newport to witness the first race of the America's Cup. Almost every weekend and on Wednesday afternoons, the crew took the schooner out for a cruise. During the fall and spring terms, the *Tabor Boy* visited such places as Mystic, Newport, Nantucket, Marblehead, Hingham and other ports. At the end of fall

Gordon Goodwin, left, a Marion boy, prepares a shell for practice along with the rest of the 1963 Tabor varsity 8 crew, under the guidance of coach Harry C. Hoyle.

season, there was a rough passage from New Bedford to Charleston, S.C. where she remained for the winter months. During the spring vacation the crew cruised from Charleston to Nassau and returned to New Bedford the first week in April. Much time and effort have gone into making the schooner an even better training ship this year. One prominent improvement was the addition of a new square sail, changing the rig of the vessel to that of a square topsail schooner.

In 1960, the schooner cruised more than 1,000 miles on weekend trips to Portland, Nantucket, Newport, and Provincetown. It cruised to Charleston, South Carolina, for winter storage and then on to Nassau for its annual Spring Cruise. Improvements to the boat that year included a hand-carved golden eagle for the stern, a new radio direction finder, and the rebuilding of the anchor winch.

In 1985, Headmaster Peter Webster announced a "new program" for the 92-foot ocean-cruising schooner *Tabor Boy* called "An Education at Sea." Cruises "would be operating in Southern waters during the winter for the purpose of providing a series of two-week sail-training/'outward-bound' type experiences for Tabor students." In preparation for the new program, *Tabor Boy* was taken out of service and given a complete refit. She then returned to the waters in "superb condition" and was transferred to Fort Lauderdale, Florida, in early January for the two-week cruises. Participating students stood regular watches and performed crew functions such as manning the sails and "swabbing the decks." In addition to on-board experience, there was an exploration of local ecology and historical sites ashore during the voyages. The schooner operated out of Fort Lauderdale and sailed to the Bahamas and the surrounding islands. One of the focal points was the castle on Whatling's Island, or Little San Salvador, where students investigated the flora and fauna and surrounding waters.

Over the years, students at Tabor have experienced the unique opportunities offered by the *Tabor Boy*. The 1994 yearbook reported on the boat's 40th anniversary at Tabor: "With each sea journey, the crew of the *Tabor Boy* experiences the excitement of new challenges, a renewed appreciation of the power of the sea, a treasured sense of camaraderie and a heightened sense of self-respect. The legacy of the *Tabor Boy* is self-discovery and pride." In 2000, the academy's yearbook said of the *Tabor Boy*, "Countless students have stood on her decks and witnessed the sheer grace with which she moves, while maintaining the vigilance and the discipline that is necessary. What a great asset this vessel is to the school and the infinite lessons learned and the adventures by all those who participate in the program."

Tabor also offered small boat instruction and racing for its students. In 1940, E-boats were raced. In 1955, Tabor offered a fall sailing program and a competitive spring program, winning the New England Prep Championship. That same year, John Rolfe and Don McPherson won the New England Interscholastic Dinghy Championship. The 1957 yearbook depicts Tabor students racing in the two-

Tabor girls are shown here aboard the Tabor Boy *in 1929.*

Female students wear their Tabor uniforms in 1926.

person Mercury class, while the 1961 yearbook includes the race results of the Puffin, Mercury, and Wood Pussy classes (Gordon Goodwin of Marion won the Mercury class that year). In addition, new Cottontails and Jet 14s provided training in planing-type hulls.

In 1959, three races were held every week in the Mercury, Puffin, and Wood Pussy classes and series winners received either the Angier Trophy or the Braitmayer Trophy. The coaches instilled in the boys that sailboat racing was a game requiring exceptional integrity and sportsmanship and that teamwork in sailing was very delicate and often required self-sacrifice. In 1968, Silver Terns were added for the fall sailing program. Coach Maxwell pronounced that the 1968 season would be remembered for its sportsmanship, teamwork, and victories. In 1969, a new high-performance sailboat, the *International Tempest*, was added to Tabor's program along with another quick-planing boat, the *International 505*. Tabor's program had both depth and breadth in that it was not only able to teach inexperienced sailors to sail, but also had a competitive racing program of the highest caliber. Intramural races were held in Terns, Wood Pussies, Puffins, Jets, and Cottontails. In 1972, the Shields class boat was added; in 1975, Lasers (one-person planing boats); and in 1977, Bunny Boats.

In competition, Tabor students proved skilled and determined. The members of the 1975 Tabor varsity sailing team were the New England champions and won the New England School Sailing Association (NESSA) Team Championships. In 1976, Tabor achieved first place in the Annual Naval Academy Regatta. In 1977, it won the NESSA Regatta (1st of 19) and the Mallory Trophy Regatta (1st of 19 and Best Skipper) in 420s, and in 1978, the O'Day/Mallory Cup (1st of 14) also in 420s, which has been the racing class ever since.

When Tabor became co-educational in 1980, female students began to participate in the sailing program. In 1996, the co-ed sailing team had a 12-0 record, and the 420 squad was led by Megan Edwards and Dan Herlihy. The yearbook stated, "The Seawolves won the O'Day Regatta, New England Fleet Championship, placed 2nd in the Mallory Regatta in Annapolis and won the Interscholastic Sailing Association (ISSA) Fleet Championship. Tabor went to the Baker Regatta, ISSA Team Championship in San Francisco and finished second, losing an exciting race to Newport Harbor, CA."

In 1999, the "Tabor Sailing Seawolves closed the millennium as one of the most dominant sailing teams in the school's history." The team won the New England Sailing "triple crown" backed up by a 19-0 regular season (earning the most wins in one season). In October of that year, co-captain Joel Hanneman also won the single-handed title. In April 2000, the Seawolves won the fleet championship with 35 points more than their closest competitor and in early May, Tabor earned its

A coed sailing team competes in an interscholastic regatta. Tabor's Seawolves were consistent national champions under coach Toby Baker, who retired in 1999.

Tabor students are dressed for graduation in 1926.

13th team racing title in 14 years. The team's revered coach Toby Baker retired that year after a wonderful career. Under his coaching, the Tabor Sailing Team won the NESSA Team Championship 1996–1997 and 1999–2000; NESSA Fleet Championship 1992, 1993, 1995, 1996, 1999, and 2000; ISSA Team Championship, 1989–1991 and 1994; and the British Schools Dinghy Racing Association Championship, 1990 and 1995.

It did not take long either for the first class of female students to build successful crew teams. The 1980 Girls Crew was 0-4 in its first season, but by 1988 they emerged as the best in New England, receiving first place in the New England championships. They also competed at the Women's Royal Henley Regatta in England in 1997 and 1999.

Over the years Tabor has formed other clubs and extracurricular activities related to the sea. The 1957 yearbook explains that the "Navigation Club was formed to provide a program for students who wished to pursue further their interest in naval science and naval history. At their meetings, members present research findings on appropriate topics, reports that are generally followed by informal discussions concerning naval science. In 1957, most of the members are leading sailors on the *Tabor Boy*." Also, "In order to qualify as a candidate for membership, a student must have completed two years of Naval Science." By 1964, the Navigation Club had 50 members and hosted such speakers as George

O'Day, an Olympic sailor, and Ralph Thatcher of Cape Cod Shipbuilding, a major sailboat builder.

The Boat Shop group was organized in 1956 and by 1958 the yearbook stated,

> The accomplishments of the Boat Shop this past winter should be highly commended. Special recognition is due Capt. Glaeser and Bryant Palmer for their leadership and perseverance . . . The main job that confronts the boys each winter is getting the Mercuries and catboats in shape for spring sailing and for the summer camp. This year special attention was devoted to the renovation of the *Argo* which was in need of much work.

In the following year, the group renovated the shop, took down the sail racks to increase the working area, and performed the "fiberglassing of six Mercuries and two Cats." Other boats were sanded down and painted, and three launches were worked into shape. In 1965, the Boat Shop had completed maintenance on the Cottontails, Terns, Wood Pussies, and Puffins. Over the years, other clubs were added from time to time, including a Diving Club, Fish Club, and a Tabor Yacht Club, and cruising boats were also added, including *Serendipity*, *Landfall*, *Elizabeth Taber*, and *Sea Wind*.

In 1966, an Oceanography Project was organized at Tabor to help students "learn the fundamentals of oceanography," and in 1978, the Department of Marine Sciences was started. Today students at Tabor may enroll in advanced oceanology, Advanced Placement environmental studies, astronomy, meteorology, and reef ecology, in addition to courses in biology, chemistry, and physics. They

Headmaster Walter Huston Lillard designed Tabor's seal in 1916 to commemorate the reorganization of the school. The motto "all-a-taut-o" is a nautical term meaning "everything shipshape and ready to run," which Lillard took as his inspiration in running the school.

may also take a seamanship course or just work on an individual project such as seeding and growing oysters in cultivated beds. Because of its unique location, Tabor also offers courses in the nautical sciences including navigation, piloting and seamanship, naval architecture, and maritime history.

Jay S. Stroud, the academy's current headmaster, describes Tabor today in the following way: "Our unparalleled location on the edge of the sea creates our metaphor for education. While some of our students literally study marine biology or celestial navigation, sail boats both large and small, row crew shells or swim off Tabor's docks, all our students undertake voyages of the mind and spirit." He believes that Tabor "reminds us all daily that life is about the largest visions possible. It is about widening the horizon, redefining the possible, developing the courage to undertake great voyages. All of us who live here are fortunate to have both the joy and the possibility of adventure in the tides that rise at our front door every morning. It is the right place for a school." The Tabor class motto from 1899, "Row, not drift," still applies to the school by the sea today.

This is a view of Tabor Academy from Sippican Harbor.

14. MARION-TO-BERMUDA CRUISING YACHT RACE

On June 25, 1977, the first Marion-to-Bermuda Cruising Yacht Race was held. This 645-mile offshore race was sponsored by the Blue Water Sailing Club and the Royal Hamilton Amateur Dinghy Club. As the story is told, the biennial Marion-to-Bermuda Cruising Yacht Race, which is held in alternate years from the Newport-to-Bermuda Ocean Yacht Race, began as a casual conversation in the Caribbean. According to Trudy Kingery, "We were sailing, my husband and I, in the Caribbean with [Bermuda's] Dickie Bird and they were talking about racing, so we said, 'Let's race from our house to your house.' Our house is in Marion and his is in Bermuda . . . that's how it got started." The first race had 104 starters. Unlike the Newport-to-Bermuda Race, which attracts highly competitive ocean racers, the Marion-Bermuda Race attracts sailors who love to sail with family and friends, who want to enjoy racing, and who do not want to buy a new up-to-date competitive boat every two years to be able to stay in the sport.

The initial rules of the race emphasized safety and required each yacht owner to sign a seaworthiness certificate. Each entry was to carry 10 gallons of fresh water per person, have enough fuel to motor 200 miles, and store enough food for the crew for two weeks. They were also required to carry an Emergency Position Indicating Radio Beacon (EPIRB) but could not carry other radio aids such as sophisticated electronic gear, satellite receivers, and weather fax mapmakers, or weather teleprinters.

Today, the objectives of the race remain the same as they were in 1977, "to provide an opportunity for cruising yachts and amateur crews to participate in an ocean race and a rendezvous in Bermuda. It encourages the development of blue water sailing skills on seaworthy boats that can be handled safely offshore with limited crew." The participating yachts must be single-hulled, have an enclosed cabin, and be fitted out for comfortable cruising. Yachts must be between 32 feet and 62 feet long and be seaworthy and appropriate for offshore sailing. In addition, the yacht may not be designed or used primarily for racing or to further a commercial or trade purpose. Spinnakers may not be used. Because of the prevalence of electronics today, the race is divided into two divisions: a "celestial" division and an "electronic" division to accommodate navigation preferences.

The two founders of the Marion-to-Bermuda Cruising Yacht Race are David Kingery, left, and Geoffrey "Dickie" Bird, right. Race chairman John Braitmayer is in center.

In the initial year in 1977, the race was slow in light southwesterlies and most of the officials at the finish line expected *Chee Chee* to cross first. But her position proved not to be accurate and *Silkie* appeared out of the blue to take line honors, first on corrected time, and first shorthanded.

In 1979, the second year of the race, the Beverly Yacht Club was added as a sponsor. There were 128 starters that plunged into 25-knot southwesterlies, and the struggle with nature caused two dismastings and 14 DNFs (did not finish). *Silkie* won the shorthanded trophy, while *Gabriella* took first to finish and first on corrected time. A new family trophy was created and awarded to *Asteroid*.

In 1981, 143 starters crossed the line. Not long into the race the wind picked up and by the halfway mark had turned into 45 knots of howling trouble. Thirty-eight boats did not finish, mainly due to gear problems. And despite safety precautions, the fleet's scratch boat, the Britton Chance–designed, lightweight-displacement cutter *Satan's Mercy* was holed and sank in the Gulf Stream. The boat lost its mast, and as the crew began to cut away the tangle of rigging, they noticed a 10-by-15-inch hole at the water line. No one knows whether the yacht hit a log while beating to windward in the dark or whether the spreader punched a hole in the side as it came tumbling down with the mast. Her entire eight-man crew was later rescued by another competitor, *Wind Burn*, whose crew then elected to carry on with the race. Because of calms near Bermuda, *Wind Burn*'s food supply ran out and she powered in. Fifteen other vessels were so late finishing that the Race Committee was no longer at St. David's to take their time.

Sly Mongoose took line honors; *Edelweiss,* first corrected; *Silkie*, first shorthanded; and the family trophy went to *Legend*. A famous participant in the race was former CBS news anchorman Walter Cronkite, sailing *Wyntie*, a class B Westsail 42 yacht.

In 1983, there were 135 yachts that started the race. Ron Noonan's *Wildflower*, from class G, won first overall, while Herb Marcus again took honors sailing shorthanded in *Silkie*. *Asteroid* again won the family trophy.

In 1985, participation was down to 110 yachts as light air from the south dogged the fleet almost down to Bermuda, where on Wednesday morning a massive southwester blew in. The winners reached the finish from the west, but most of the fleet beat into repetitive thunderstorms. *Carioca* and *Fleetwing* were dismasted, with *Fleetwing* finally abandoned. Twenty-two boats withdrew, but *Pirate* stole the show on corrected time not far behind *Charisma*'s first to finish. The shorthanded trophy went to *Silkie*, and *Legend* got the family prize.

In 1987, a fleet of 149 yachts started the race. Most classes started with a southwesterly wind of 25 knots, and all classes got away cleanly with no premature starts, no fouls, and no protests. Unfortunately, there was one serious accident outside the starting area. Early in the afternoon, a 40-foot sloop was dismasted in a collision with a 40-foot cutter. The collision occurred before the

H.D. Marcus's Silkie *was first overall and first to finish in the 1977 race.*

starting sequences began for either boat. Nobody was hurt, but the sloop was towed to a boatyard in Marion. The cutter sustained only minimal damage and continued the race. The 59-foot class A cutter *Runaway*, with a family crew of four from Lyme, Connecticut, took line honors, completing the race in 80 hours. *Runaway* benefited from the strong winds in the frontal weather system that produced the fastest Marion-Bermuda Race to date. *Legend* took class B silverware along with the family trophy. Kevin Carse of Guilford; his wife, Lorraine; two sons, Kevin Jr., 18, and Thomas, 16; Kevin Sr.'s brother George; and family friend Bub Gulomb credited their win to long experience sailing to Bermuda, especially across the tricky Gulf Stream.

The start of the 1989 race suffered several postponements due to a lack of adequate wind. However, once the race was underway, 163 vessels, the biggest fleet yet, cleared the starting line and headed for Bermuda. *War Baby* of Bermuda crossed the finish line after 72.5 hours at sea, eclipsing the previous record by almost two hours. Corrected time honors went to John Elliot's 34-foot class F sloop *Yukon Jack*, which was followed closely by Blue Water Sailing Club Commodore Jim Hayes's 40-foot class E sloop *Shambles*. One hundred forty-five yachts finished the race.

Entries for the 1991 race were down from the record 1989 fleet with just 117 vessels starting on what was a beautiful day in Marion. But when the fleet entered the Gulf Stream, it was met with a storm from the northeast, purportedly having a radius of some 300 miles. With winds gusting to near hurricane force, the stream quickly became a maelstrom of confused seas running between 30 and 40 feet.

Class B starts in the 1979 Marion-Bermuda Race.

After struggling through many hours the fleet emerged from the stream into relatively quiet waters. A tribute to the preparations and seamanship of the participants was the fact that there were no major mishaps. Corrected time honors went to Richard Carleton's class E Pearson 36 *Orion*, followed very closely by Morris Kellog's class F Shannon 43 *Blue Magic*. The Bavier Seamanship/Sportsman Trophy was awarded to Francis Checkoski for his outstanding performance bringing his vessel safely into Bermuda.

The ninth Marion-Bermuda Race in 1993 had 115 entries. At starting time, the typical Buzzards Bay sou'wester kicked in and winds were estimated to be 20 to 30 knots. This year, the entire bay was shrouded in thick fog resulting in a collision that caused the retirement of two vessels. The fleet's passage down Buzzards Bay tested the navigational skills and the mettle of all participants. Several groundings and near misses were reported, but by nightfall all yachts had cleared "Sow and Pigs." The passage through the Gulf Stream and on to Bermuda presented a near idyllic sail, from all reports. The Bermuda vessel *Alphida*, skippered by Kirk Cooper, claimed line honors and despite light winds off Bermuda set a new Marion-Bermuda course record. Corrected time honors went to Ron Noonan's class G *Wildflower*, his third First in Class award. Noonan, a member of the Beverly Yacht Club, described his approach to this race:

> I divide the race into three segments, each of which requires a different strategy. The beat out of the Bay, although a small part of the race, is often quite decisive. You might get out with a five minute gain if you do things right, but this is a big psychological lift for the crew. You use "around the buoys" strategies going down the Bay, watching the currents and the wind, and there are geological shifts as well. Almost everybody ends up playing the shores, but it's not automatic. The second segment is from Sow and Pigs to the Stream. Here, you're trying to enter the Stream at the proper point and also cash in on any eddys you encounter along the way. You'll still have to watch the vicissitudes of the weather, though. The third segment runs from your exit from the Stream to the finish. This is 60 percent of the race. Projecting what the wind is going to do and how to take advantage of it are the skills for this segment. When you're inside the 50 mile mark, going for the barn is a very strong temptation, but it's been my experience that when you get close to Bermuda, the wind generally backs to the south-southwest, so it's often wise to keep some windward money in the bank.

In 1995, 77 entries cleared the starting line in perfect weather for a fast sail down Buzzards Bay. However, two vessels experienced rigging problems and were forced in for repairs. By dusk, all racers had cleared the bay. Upon arrival at the Gulf Stream, participants discovered conditions that were truly uncharacteristic. For more than 16 hours, a dead calm persisted while the entire fleet drifted off to the east. The arrival of wind found the fleet completely together, leading to the start of a virtually new race for the next 300 miles to St. David's Head. Dick Leather's *Columbine* claimed first to finish honors. On corrected time, Carter Cordner's Westsail 32 *Kemancha* claimed the overall winner's trophy, denying Ron Noonan's *Wildflower* a "hat trick" by less than 30 minutes. The Bavier Seamanship/Sportsmanship Trophy was not awarded this year; however, the crew of *Spinache* did receive a certificate of merit for their commendable act of seamanship in stopping to investigate and salvage the log and personal effects from an abandoned yacht in the Gulf Stream.

In 1997, the 20th anniversary of the Marion-to-Bermuda Cruising Yacht Race, there were 84 starters. This year's skippers had the option of utilizing unrestricted electronics, but for those who elected to navigate the old-fashioned way, a 3 percent bonus was added to their time allowance. Interestingly, about 75 percent of the entries chose to make the passage relying solely on star sights and dead reckoning. Time honors went to *Akka*, skippered by Alex Rosenbladt of Atlantic Highlands, New Jersey. Overall first place on corrected time went to one of the smallest vessels in the fleet, *Majek*, skippered by Abbot Fletcher of Bath, Maine. This more-than-30-year-old vessel, crewed by the Fletcher family, illustrated that a well-sailed classic design can compete in any arena.

The 1999 race, with 103 starters, established two separate divisions for navigators. Though the race was originally limited to those skippers and crews who steered by the stars, as the use of electronics became more popular race organizers offered a celestial navigation division and one for sailors who use modern electronics. Race organizers were concerned that the celestial component would gradually disappear if they did not take supportive action. The fleet was equally divided into six electronic or celestial classes. The race began with an unusual downwind start with winds of 18 to 20 knots from the northeast. Through a variety of tactics the fleet negotiated Buzzards Bay and by nightfall was on course towards the Gulf Stream. First overall went to *Dakota*, a Swan 46 skippered by Doug Ely, and first to finish went to *Temptress*, skippered by Richard Shulman.

The 2001 race was the slowest in the race's 24-year history. It was so slow that 26 boats withdrew, leaving only 53 boats to finish in the light 5–7 knot air and calm seas. The first boat finished two days later than the first boats normally would finish in previous competitions. On several becalmed boats, crews took swims in the ocean. *Veritas*, a Frers 46 and captained by Phil Hutchinson from Harwood, Maryland, was the first to finish. He commented, "We attribute this to the crew and being a little lucky. We were 100 miles east of the rhumbline and we were nervous about our position, but the boat was always pointing toward Bermuda." Two years previous, *Veritas* finished dead last. Of the turnaround, the captain said, "It's euphoric to go from 'tail-end Charlie' to the first in the fleet."

The late W. David Kingery, chairman of the Blue Water Cruising Yacht Race Committee, wrote of the race, "This race was conceived . . . as a contest among offshore cruising yachts with cruising-style crews racing toward a pleasant rendezvous where one can raft together and relax with new and old friends. That

J.W. Braitmayer's ketch Karina *was co-winner of the Bermuda Longtail Trophy in 1979.* Karina *also won the Family Trophy in 1993.*

is our objective." The intent behind the Marion-Bermuda Race was to allow older but still seaworthy yachts a chance at real blue water racing with a family aboard. The race employs the Measurement Handicap System, one of a variety of handicapping systems used in offshore racing to even out yachts that vary widely in shape, size, and speed. The race from Marion to Bermuda usually takes four or five days depending on the wind.

The following is a list of the race results beginning with the first year of the Marion-to-Bermuda Race:

1977 (104 STARTERS)

First Overall	*Silkie,* H.D. Marcus
First to Finish	*Silkie,* H.D. Marcus
First Shorthanded	*Silkie,* H.D. Marcus
Navigator's Trophy	H.D. Marcus

First, Class A	*Insurgente*, U.S. Naval Academy
First, Class B	*Silkie*, H.D. Marcus
First, Class C	*Frolic*, U.S. Naval Academy
First, Class D	*Robin Too*, K.D. Empacher
First, Class E	*Hollimar*, R. Goldsmith
First, Class F	*Dawn Piper*, C.L. Steedman
First, Class G	*Sixpence*, H.P. Bakewell Jr.
Corporation of Hamilton Trophy	*Asteroid*, A.E. Doughty
Adams Trophy	*Tioga*, P.P. Noyes
Naval Academy Trophy	*Insurgente*, U.S. Naval Academy
Commodores' Cup	*Robin Too*, K.D. Empacher
Town of Marion Trophy	*Blue Pidgeon*, M.A. Gordon

1979 (128 STARTERS)

First Overall	*Gabriella*, H.P. Clayman
First to Finish	*Gabriella*, H.P. Clayman
First Shorthanded	*Astri*, W.K. Foss
First Family	*Asteroid*, A.E. Doughty Sr.
Navigator's Trophy	H.P. Clayman
First, Class A	*Ayesha*, J. Butterfield
First, Class B	*Gabriella*, H P. Clayman
First, Class C	*Argonaut*, A.L. Friedman

J.D. Cochran's 53-foot sloop Sly Mongoose IV *was first to finish in the 1981 and 1983 races.*

First, Class D	*Isolde*, J.H. Westerbeke Jr.
First, Class E	*Wind Flower II*, H.L. Everett
First, Class F	*Astri*, W.K. Foss
First, Class G	*Damn Yankee*, R.F. Deluca
Corporation of Hamilton Trophy	*Velvet Paws*, J.V. Gardner
Adams Trophy	*Wind Flower II*, H.L. Everett
Naval Academy Trophy	*Jen*, W.W. Ross
Commodores' Cup	*Isolde*, J.H. Westerbeke Jr.
Town of Marion Trophy	*White Caps*, H. White
Bermuda Longtail Trophy	*Wild Flower* and *Karina*
Seamanship/Sportsman Award	W.D. Kingery

1981 (143 STARTERS)

First Overall	*Edelweis*, A.J. Shatkin
First to Finish	*Sly Mongoose IV*, J.D. Cochran
First Shorthanded	*Silkie*, H.D. Marcus
First Family	*Legend*, K.J. Carse
Navigator's Trophy	N. Nicholson
First, Class A	*Sly Mongoose IV*, J.D. Cochran
First, Class B	*Silkie*, H.D. Marcus
First, Class C	*White Caps*, H. White
First, Class D	*Caper*, J. Charnok
First, Class E	*Edelweis*, A.J. Shatkin
First, Class F	*Harrier*, J. Bontecou
First, Class G	*Wizard*, J.E. McHutchinson Jr.
Corporation of Hamilton Trophy	*Asteroid*, A.E. Doughty
Adams Trophy	*White Caps*, H. White
Naval Academy Trophy	*Foxy Lady*, R. Fox
Commodores' Cup	*Keramos*, W.D. Kingery
Town of Marion Trophy	*Transit*, E.E. Bensley
Bermuda Longtail Trophy	*Curlew*, E.C. Brainard, II
Seamanship/Sportsman Award	R.F. Biebel and crew of *Windburn*

1983 (135 STARTERS)

First Overall	*Wild Flower*, R.P. Noonan
First to Finish	*Sly Mongoose IV*, J.D. Cochran
First Shorthanded	*Silkie*, H.D. Marcus
First Family	*Asteroid*, A.E. Doughty Sr.
Navigator's Trophy	David Johns
First, Class A	*Carioca*, J. Domenie
First, Class B	*Cygne*, R.S. Peterson
First, Class C	*Silkie*, H.D. Marcus

First, Class D	*Querencia*, C.C. Cunningham
First, Class E	*Galivant*, L. Rittenberg
First, Class F	*Clarion*, W.L. and S.P. Gray
First, Class G	*Wild Flower*, R.P. Noonan
Corporation of Hamilton Trophy	*Nimue*, J.V. Gardner
Adams Trophy	*Clarion*, W.L. and S.P. Gray
Naval Academy Trophy	*Galivant*, L. Rittenberg
Commodores Cup	*Sea Nest*, G.E. Michaud
Town of Marion Trophy	*Bienestar*, C.M. Reppert
Bermuda Longtail Trophy	*Keramos*, W.D. Kingery

1985 (110 STARTERS)

First Overall	*Pirate*, M.C. Mehlburger
First to Finish	*Charisma*, R. Beres
First Shorthanded	*Silkie*, H.D. Marcus
First Family	*Legend*, K. Carse Sr.
Navigator's Trophy	N. Nicholson
First, Class A	*Runaway*, P. D'Arcy
First, Class B	*Alert*, R. Armstrong
First, Class C	*Silkie*, H.D. Marcus
First, Class D	*La Difference*, W. Jensen
First, Class E	*Pirate*, M.C. Mehlburger
First, Class F	*Trilogy*, J. Barr
First, Class G	*Wildflower*, R. Noonan
Corporation of Hamilton Trophy	*Asteroid*, A.E. Doherty
Adams Trophy	*Chouette*, A. DeSatnick
Naval Academy Trophy	*Alert*, R. Armstrong
Commodores' Cup	*No Se*, D. Marshall
Town of Marion Trophy	*Wildflower*, R. Noonan
Bermuda Longtail Trophy	*Clarion*, S.P. and W.L. Gray Jr.
Seamanship/Sportsman Award	Thomas Warner and Peter Kenny of the yacht *Carioca* and the Air-Sea Rescue Team of the U.S. Naval Air Station, Bermuda

1987 (149 STARTERS)

First Overall	*Legend*, K.J. Carse Jr.
First to Finish	*Runaway*, P. D'Arcy
First Shorthanded	*Astri*, W.K. Foss
First Family	*Legend*, K.J. Carse Jr.
Navigator's Trophy	K.J. Carse Jr.
First, Class A	*Shortz*, K. Bosch

First, Class B	*Legend*, K.J. Carse Jr.
First, Class C	*White Caps*, H. White
First, Class D	*Invictus*, J. Ellis
First, Class E	*Pirate*, M.C. Mehlburger
First, Class F	*Astri*, W.K. Foss
First, Class G	*Encore*, E. Waldman
Corporation of Hamilton Trophy	*Shortz*, K. Bosch
Adams Trophy	*Encore*, E. Waldman
Naval Academy Trophy	*Constellation*, D. Whitney
Commodores' Cup	*Shambles*, J. Hayes
Town of Marion Trophy	*White Caps*, H. White
Bermuda Longtail Trophy	*Horizon*, J. Noble

W.L. and S.P. Gray's Clarion *was first in class F in 1983 and won the Adams Trophy. In 1985 she won the Bermuda Longtail Trophy.*

Deborah Anne Domenie Trophy   *Invictus*, J. Ellis
Seamanship/Sportsman Award   Paul Nelson, Skipper of *Jeunesse*

1989 (163 STARTERS)

First Overall	*Yukon Jack*, J. Elliott
First to Finish	*War Baby*, W.A. Brown
First Shorthanded	*Yukon Jack*, J. Elliott
First Family	*Wind's Way*, S.&J. MacFarlan
Navigator's Trophy	T. Plummer
First, Class A	*Chasseur*, F.V. Snyder
First, Class B	*Akka*, A.E. Rosenblad
First, Class C	*Aurora*, E. Tarlov
First, Class D	*Snow White*, E.A. Shuman
First, Class E	*Shambles*, J.E. Hayes
First, Class F	*Yukon Jack*, J. Elliott
First, Class G	*Primma Donna*, D. Puchkoff
Corporation of Hamilton Trophy	*Tonka*, P. Hubbard
Adams Trophy	*Shambles*, J.E. Hayes

Norman Shachoy's Volunteer *from Marion starts the tenth Marion-to-Bermuda Race on June 16, 1995.*

Naval Academy Trophy	*Snow White*, E.A. Shuman
Commodores' Cup	*Gannet*, J. Fantasia
Town of Marion Trophy	*Volunteer*, N.J. Shachoy
Bermuda Longtail Trophy	*Prospect of Whitby*, C.A. McDonald
Deborah Anne Domenie Trophy	*Chasseur*, F.V. Snyder
RHADC Centennial Trophy	*Tonka*, P. Hubbard; *Distant Drum*, T.J. Dickinson; *Asteroid*, A.E. Doughty Sr.

1991 (117 STARTERS)

First Overall	*Orion*, R.A. Carleton
First to Finish	*Alphida*, E.K. Cooper
First Shorthanded	*Aquoreal II*, P. Rasmussen
First Family	*Sinn Fein*, P.S. Robovich
Navigator's Trophy	*Orion*, R. Norton
First, Class A	*Integrity*, P.&D. Wendel
First, Class B	*Sharone*, E.H. Brown
First, Class C	*Volante*, R.B. Womsley
First, Class D	*Sinn Fein*, P.S. Rebovich
First, Class E	*Orion*, R.A. Carleton
First, Class F	*Blue Magic*, M.W. Kellog
First, Class G	*Kitty Hawk*, G. Sanford
Corporation of Hamilton Trophy	*Tonka*, P.B. Hubbard
Adams Trophy	*Blue Magic*, M.W. Kellog
Naval Academy Trophy	*Snow White*, E.A. Shuman
Commodores' Cup	*Shambles*, J.E. Hayes
Town of Marion Trophy	*Kitty Hawk*, G. Sanford
Bermuda Longtail Trophy	*Prospect of Whitby*, D. McDonald
Deborah Anne Domenie Trophy	*Sharone*, E.H. Brown
RHADC Centennial Trophy	*Blue Magic*, M.W. Kellog; *Schedar*, P.D. Haddock; *Arcadia Orca*, B. Emory
Seamanship/Sportsman Award	Paul Nelson, Skipper of *Jeunesse*

1993 (115 STARTERS)

First Overall	*Wildflower*, R. Noonan
First to Finish	*Alphida*, E.K. Cooper
First Shorthanded	*Xapiema*, R.I. Walsh
First Family	*Karina*, J.W. Braitmayer
Navigator's Trophy	*Wildflower*, R. Noonan & K. Reed
First, Class A	*Tsunami*, B. Rego
First, Class B	*Panama Red*, R. Bioty

First, Class C	*Frodo*, J.G. Stegle
First, Class D	*White Caps*, H. White
First, Class E	*Dear Friend*, B. Kardash
First, Class F	*Majek*, A. Fletcher
First, Class G	*Wildflower*, R. Noonan
Corporation of Hamilton Trophy	*Tonka*, P. Hubbard
Adams Trophy	*Majek*, A. Fletcher
Naval Academy Trophy	*Restless*, E.W. Crawford
Commodores' Cup	*Zephyr*, J. Noble
Town of Marion Trophy	*Kitty Hawk*, G. Sanford
Bermuda Longtail Trophy	*Clarion*, S.&L. Gray
Deborah Anne Domenie Trophy	*Next Boat*, M. Ellman
The Bartrum Trophy	*Vigilant*, T. Kelly
RHADC Centennial Trophy	*Karina*, J.W. Braitmayer; *Tsunami*, B. Rego; *Lullaby*, D.N Roblin

1995 (77 STARTERS)

First Overall	*Kemancha*, C. Cordner
First to Finish	*Columbine*, R.B. Leather
First Shorthanded	*Shooting Star*, D. Kingsbury
First Family	*Xapiema*, R. Welsh
Navigator's Trophy	*Kemancha*, J. Hackett
First, Class A	*Veritas*, P. Hutchinson Jr.
First, Class B	*Swift*, G. Huss
First, Class C	*Cracker Jack*, A. Krulish
First, Class D	*North Star*, G. M. Rouzee
First, Class E	*Xapiema*, R. Welsh Jr.
First, Class F	*Kemancha*, C. Cordner
Corporation of Hamilton Trophy	*Tonka*, P. Hubbard
Adams Trophy	*Wildflower*, R. Noonan
Naval Academy Trophy	*Restless*, E.W. Crawford
Commodores' Cup	*Allegro*, D. Atwood
Town of Marion Trophy	*Volunteer II*, Paul Skipper
Bermuda Longtail Trophy	*Zephyr II*, J. Noble
Deborah Anne Domenie Trophy	*Spinache*, J. Laeless
The Bartrum Trophy	*Swift*, G. Huss
RHADC Centennial Trophy	*Allegro*, D. Atwood; *Windborne*, N. Doelling; *Zephyr II*, J. Noble

1997 (84 STARTERS)

First Overall	*Majek*, A. Fletcher
First to Finish	*Akka*, A. Rosenbladt

Yachts rendezvous in Bermuda after the race.

First Shorthanded	*Next Boat*, M. Ellman
First Family	*Impala*, A. Sanford
Navigator's Trophy	*Majek*, M. Fletcher
First, Class A	*Akka*, A. Rosenbladt
First, Class B	*Veritas*, P. Hutchinson
First, Class C	*Cracker Jack*, A. Krulish
First, Class D	*Cadence*, W. Taylor
First, Class E	*Anny*, L. Vultree
First, Class F	*Majek*, A. Fletcher
Corporation of Hamilton Trophy	*Tonka*, P. Hubbard
Adams Trophy	*Patriot*, D. Hyland
Naval Academy Trophy	*Veritas*, P. Hutchinson
Commodores' Cup	*Fastacks*, H. Stacks
Town of Marion Trophy	*Wildflower*, R. Noonan
Bermuda Longtail Trophy	*Zephyr II*, J. Noble
Deborah Anne Domenie Trophy	*Anny*, L. Vultree
The Bartrum Trophy	*Swift*, J. Ward
RHADC Centennial Trophy	*Carina*, R. Potts; *Skylight*, P. Shuwall; *Symphony*, J. Mertz

Bettina Unhoch is on the Sly Mongoose *at the beginning of the Marion-to-Bermuda Race.*

1999 (103 STARTERS)

First Overall	*Dakota*, D. Ely
First to Finish	*Temptress*, R. Shulman
First Shorthanded	*Rocinante*, D. Ritchie
First Family	*Althea*, W. Ewing
Navigator's Trophy	*Flirt*, G. Mitchell
First, Class A (celestial)	*Flirt*, G. Mitchell
First, Class B (electronic)	*Dakota*, D. Ely
First, Class C (celestial)	*Cracker Jack*, A. Krulish
First, Class D (electronic)	*Acadia*, B. Keenan
First, Class E (celestial)	*Majek*, A. Fletcher
First, Class F (electronic)	*Lelek*, R. Bernert
Corporation of Hamilton Trophy	*Babe*, Dr. C. Couper
Adams Trophy	*Wildflower*, R. Noonan
Naval Academy Trophy	*Cracker Jack*, A. Krulish
Commodores' Cup	*Levanter*, P. Goldberg
Town of Marion Trophy	*Zephyr II*, J. Noble
Bermuda Longtail Trophy	*Hawke*, Dr. G. Vineyard
Deborah Anne Domenie Trophy	*Scaramouche*, F. Bauerschmidt

The Bartram Trophy   *Vigilant*, R. Almeida
Ocean Spray Team Trophy   U.S. Naval Academy Sailing

2001 (79 STARTERS)

First Overall   *Spinache*, J. Lawless
First to Finish   *Veritas*, P. Hutchinson
First Shorthanded (electronic)   *Solace*, D. Owen
First Shorthanded (celestial)   *Panacea*, G. MacDonald
First Family (electronic)   *Rhapsody*, M. Asaro
First Family (celestial)   *Solution*, C. Bacon Jr.
Navigator's Trophy   *Spinche*, R. Graham
First, Class A (celestial)   *Wildflower*, R. Noonan
First, Class A (electronic)   *Despedida*, N. Cannistraro
First, Class B (celestial)   *Spinache*, J. Lawless
First, Class B (electronic)   *Veritas*, P. Hutchinson
First, Class C (electronic)   *Kitty Hawk*, G. Sanford
First, Class D (electronic)   *Solace*, D. Owen
Corporation of Hamilton Trophy   *Bermuda Oyster*, P. Hubbard
Adams Trophy   *Seaflower*, R. Chevrier
Naval Academy Trophy   *Despedida*, N. Cannistraro
Commodores' Cup   *Fiddlers Green*, D. Patton and
                                                          J. Noble

Town of Marion Trophy   *Kitty Hawk*, G. Sanford
Deborah Anne Domenie Trophy   *Sinn Fein*, P. Rebovich
Bermuda Longtail Trophy   *Wildflower*, R. Noonan
The Bartram Trophy   *Lively*, M. Smith
Ocean-Spray Team Trophy   *Harrasseket Yacht Club*

The Marion-to-Bermuda Race remains to this day a race for offshore cruising yachts with cruising-style crews. In fact, no professional crews are allowed. This type of racing fills a need for those who love to race offshore but want to do so in their own cruising boats with friends. It is fitting that this type of "blue water" racing was conceived in Marion. This community is unpretentious, sturdy, and fun and maintains its timeless values so at home on the sea.

BIBLIOGRAPHY

Allen, Everett S. *A Wind to Shake the World: The Story of the 1938 Hurricane*. Boston: Little, Brown and Company, 1976.

———. *Children of the Light: The Rise and Fall of New Bedford Whaling and the Death of the Arctic Fleet*. Boston: Little, Brown and Company, 1973.

Ashley, Clifford W. *Whaleships of New Bedford*. New York: Houghton-Mifflin Co., 1929.

Brewington, M.V. and Dorothy. *Kendall Whaling Museum Paintings*. Sharon, MA: Kendall Whaling Museum, 1965.

Bryan, George S. *Mystery Ship: The* Mary Celeste *in Fancy and in Fact*. Philadelphia and New York: J.B. Lippincott Company, 1942.

Church, Albert C. *Whale Ships and Whaling*. New York: W.W. Norton & Co., 1938.

Fay, Charles Edey. Mary Celeste: *The Odyssey of an Abandoned Ship*. Salem, MA: Peabody Museum, 1942.

Fraser, James R. *Beverly Yacht Club History*. Marion, MA: Beverly Yacht Club, 1960.

Gurney, Judith Jenney. *Tales of Old Rochester*. Baltimore: Gateway Press, Inc., 1990.

Leonard, Mary Hall, et. al. *Mattapoisett and Old Rochester Massachusetts*. 1907. Reprinted Mattapoisett, MA: Town of Mattapoisett, 1993.

Martin, Kenneth R. *Delaware Goes Whaling 1833–1845*. Greenville, DE: The Hagley Museum, 1974.

———. *Heavy Weather and Hard Luck: Portsmouth Goes Whaling*. Portsmouth, NH: Portsmouth Marine Society, 1998.

Minsinger, William Elliott, and Charles Talcott Orloff. *Hurricane Bob: August 16–August 20, 1991: A Brief History*. Blue Hill, MA: Blue Hill Meteorological Observatory, 1992.

Rosbe, Judith Westlund. *Images of America: Marion*. Charleston, SC: Arcadia Publishing, 2000.

Ryder, Alice Austin. *Lands of Sippican*. 1934. Reprinted Marion, MA: Sippican Historical Society, 1975.

Smart, Joseph J. *The School and the Sea: A History of Tabor Academy*. Marion, MA: The Tabor Academy, 1964.

Starbuck, Alexander. *History of the American Whale Fishery from its Earliest Inception to the Year 1876*. 1878. Reprinted Secaucus, NJ: Castle Books, 1989.

Survey of Federal Archives, Work Projects Administration. *Ship Registers of New Bedford, Massachusetts*. Boston: National Archives Project, 1940.

Tripp, H. Edmund. *Reflections on a Town: A Timeless Photographic and Anecdotal Record of Over Three Centuries of Marion, Massachusetts*. Marion, MA: Sippican Historical Society, 1991.

Wood, Edward F.R. Jr. *Sailing Days at Mattapoisett 1870–1960*. New Bedford, MA: Reynolds Printing, Inc., 1961.

Yachting Magazine. "Your New Boat." New York: Simon and Schuster, 1946.

Two students stand in the water in front of Tabor Academy's Dexter House dormitory on Front Street during the 1938 hurricane.

INDEX

A Shields class races in Marion's outer harbor.